Also by Lawrence Booth

Cricket: Celebrating the Modern Game
Around the World
Arm-ball to Zooter:
A Sideways Look at the Language of Cricket

CRICKET, LOVELY CRICKET?

An Addict's Guide to the World's Most
Exasperating Game

Lawrence Booth

YELLOW JERSEY PRESS
LONDON

Published by Yellow Jersey Press 2008

2 4 6 8 10 9 7 5 3 1

First published in Great Britain in 2008 by
Yellow Jersey Press
Random House, 20 Vauxhall Bridge Road,
London SW1V 2SA

www.rbooks.co.uk

Addresses for companies within The Random House Group Limited can be
found at: www.randomhouse.co.uk/offices.htm

The Random House Group Limited Reg. No. 954009

A CIP catalogue record for this book
is available from the British Library

ISBN 9780224079143

The Random House Group Limited makes every effort to ensure that the
papers used in its books are made from trees that have been legally sourced
from well-managed and credibly certified forests. Our paper procurement
policy can be found at: www.rbooks.co.uk/environment

Mixed Sources
Product group from well-managed
forests and other controlled sources
www.fsc.org Cert no. TT-COC-2139
© 1996 Forest Stewardship Council
FSC

Typeset by SX Composing DTP, Rayleigh, Essex
Printed and bound in Great Britain by
CPI Mackays, Chatham, ME5 8TD

To Alex, Francis and Ben

Sometimes, when I feel a little exhausted with it all and the world's sitting heavily on my head, I pick up a *Wisden* and read about Len Hutton's 37 in 24 minutes in Sydney in 1946.

Harold Pinter

If [AE Housman] means us to understand that cricket, and cricket alone, has prevented men from committing suicide, then their continuation on this earth seems hardly worthwhile.

Edith Sitwell

God, this is boring.

A former girlfriend

Introduction

LET'S START on the train. If you like cricket enough to be reading this book, I'm guessing you've been there yourself. You know, staring out of the window watching the world flash by when you catch sight of a green field and some men dressed in white. Admit it: you want to find out what happens next. That next ball, delivered by a complete stranger in the middle of nowhere, begins to consume you. It shouldn't, of course, but you can't help yourself. You simply have to know what the batsman does to it before the cricket match and the train go their separate ways. You're even prepared to risk a quizzical look from the passenger opposite by craning your neck to catch a glimpse. But that's the thing about the next ball. And who invented train etiquette anyway?

Your rational side kicks in, or at least it tries to. It's only a game, you tell yourself, and there must be, what, a thousand of them taking place all over the world this Saturday. Knowing the fate of the next ball is not going to change your life. Still, the bowler really is taking a long time about it. Get a move on, mate. You try to lighten the mood by rolling your eyes at your co-passenger, who averts his. After all, one of the first rules of watching cricket from the train is that the bowler is always 60 and has a dodgy leg. *Run, for chrissake!* You mutter this a bit too loudly, but you know – *you know!* – that by the time the bowler gets to the crease you'll only be able to see the wrong half of the pitch. You'll have to work out what's happened next from the

1

reactions of the fielders and possibly the square-leg umpire, assuming he hasn't disappeared out of sight too. And what good will that be? Oh God, panic sets in. Questions swim round your head. What if the fielders are a shy lot and barely celebrate even when all three stumps are out of the ground? What if they like to appeal for everything and go up for a silly lbw, by which stage you will be able to see no more than a handful of spectators on the boundary, and who knows which side they're barracking for? Not that they're much use anyway: most of them are dozing in deckchairs. The sadder part of you, the part you would prefer to leave at home on a first date, considers the emergency handle. But by now it's too late. Face facts: the next ball will only ever be a construct of the mind.

I know you didn't see it, but how was the next ball for you? Did the batsman dead-bat it or square-cut it for four, or was he bowled offering no stroke? Because, at the risk of sounding like an American self-help manual, your decision might tell you something about the real you. If, for example, you've always reckoned yourself to be the next Kevin Pietersen, you'll have imagined a disdainful flick through midwicket. If it's Brett Lee who takes your fancy, the inswinging yorker will have come to mind. Me? I like to think the batsman became the first in the history of village cricket to be given out for obstructing the field, before hurling his bat to the ground and storming off, pausing only to give a few choice quotes to the bloke who writes the club newsletter. But then I'm a cricket journalist. You might also have guessed I'm a cricket lover too, one who will defend the game until he develops a slightly evangelical glint in his eye, or at least until the arthritic sexagenarian finally hobbles to the crease. It is a combination which means I get gently teased for being a 'fan with a laptop' by colleagues who regard any show of enthusiasm for cricket as a flaw that should disqualify you from the job of writing about it. (Hey, don't all fashion journalists hate clothes, restaurant critics loathe food and lobby correspondents detest politics?) But it is as it is, and I'm pretty sure the strange lure of the next ball will never leave me.

I won't patronise you by saying, as I unconvincingly tried to on the train, that cricket doesn't really matter enough to get sniffy about, or point out that it's just a game, which means you're supposed to enjoy it, not parse it like a piece of prose. I really do care about cricket. I also happen to know that a lot of other people care about it too. Take one of the more frantic aspects of my job. Every time I sit down to write the *Guardian* website's over-by-over commentary on England matches, usually in the small hours in our London office while the cleaner hoovers around my desk and the kettle is about to boil and Beefy and Nasser are going at each other hammer and tongs in the commentary box and Sky News is pouring out of a TV set someone forgot to switch off and the streets are quiet and I want to go to bed and I am wondering whether this cricket stuff has really gone just a bit too far – every time I sit down to write the OBO, I am inundated with emails from people all over the world who would understand instinctively what it is to crave knowledge of the next ball while the train zooms past. It is a shared passion that needs no explanation. Sometimes a glance is enough. Or in the case of long-suffering England fans, a wince.

For these emailers and me, the cliché that cricket is

more than a game can be taken as read. In fact, OBO proves that cricket can be a vehicle to air far more than your views on reverse swing. English readers revel masochistically in their side's latest mid-winter collapse in Multan or Melbourne. Indians correct my statistical errors and occasionally accuse me of being an apologist for the Old Order, when the fate of world cricket was decided over a few G&Ts at Lord's. Australians poke fun at the Poms and take offence just a little too easily, which I'm told is sadly typical of the convict mentality. And expats earning a crust in the Silicon Valley, or teaching English in the Philippines, or trekking in the Andes, or sweltering in the Congo, all tune in to partake of the sights and sounds. Leather on willow might be replaced by finger on keyboard, but the OBO is enough to convince them that cricket is always there. And it is enough to convince me that we needn't despair too much about the essential meaninglessness of sport.

Stop me if I'm sounding soppy. I don't mean to, because there are times when combining a career with a passion has its drawbacks too. A Pakistani reader once called me the C-word for querying a run-out decision. An Indian reader filled my inbox for weeks after pinning blame for all manner of British atrocities in his country firmly on my door, which is now locked and guarded twenty-four hours a day. An Australian reader took umbrage at a couple of lame gags at the expense of her beloved team by suggesting I was a 'first-class wanker'. When I wrote back to suggest otherwise – a vague approximation of the truth apparently being the first duty of every journalist – she responded with a lengthy diatribe which concluded that, when all was said and done, I was

4

basically a first-class wanker. For some, cricket really can mean too much. And when the fan-with-a-laptop part of me takes excessive pleasure from an England victory, I know I can include myself in that category. Being a journalist who is generally more concerned about filing my copy and living to write another day than whether England have won or not provides a healthy counterbalance.

But what is it about this game that even needs a counterbalance in the first place? If, like me, you have spent too much of your life checking the latest county scores on Ceefax or the internet when you think no one is looking, or picking and choosing the games that count towards your career batting average (the double century against three toddlers on Croyde beach is in; the six-ball duck against Old Cranleighans is out) then you will know that cricket addiction is the perfect excuse not to grow up. And that can be a very tempting impulse indeed. Football fans get to watch their favourite team once or twice a week for ninety minutes at a time, which means they have to find terribly adult ways of filling their remaining hours, like arguing about Christmas-tree formations and ringing Radio Five Live. Rugby followers face a similar problem, but react by wearing Barbour jackets and pulling down each other's trousers. And cricket? Cricket offers a perpetual parallel universe in which it is possible to avoid behaving like an adult until the bailiff is banging on your front door or the police have declared you a missing person. Even then, the rerun on Sky of yesterday's one-day international between New Zealand and Zimbabwe with Dave Houghton and Jeremy Coney joining Charles Colvile in the studio might have to take priority. W.G. Grace was called a 'perpetual schoolboy' by one of his biographers, and he had a huge beard. There seems little hope for the rest of us.

Consider the evidence. Test matches last five days, which means that in the equivalent of a working week your greatest concern is whether England will take the second new ball before stumps on the Saturday. The players are usually dressed in white, like a bunch of morris dancers who have lost their bells and sticks. The terminology is the stuff of playgrounds rather than pubs: never mention words like silly mid-off or googly down the Pig and Whistle, or any other hostelry with a flat roof. As for the nicknames, put it like this: Blowers, Aggers and Bearders are not forms of address serious adults should be answering to. No, cricket creates a nice little buffer zone between you and the rest of the world. It takes one look at a planet in which madmen are blowing themselves up, sea levels are rising, and *A Question of Sport* is on every night of the week, and says: 'That was missing leg, wasn't it?' It is a wilful avoidance of reality. And – if you take my arrival in the *Wisden* offices as a work-experience boy as the starting point – it has for ten years been my job to write about it. Or 'job', as most people have it.

I have loved cricket. I have resented it. I have been thrilled by it and bored witless by it. It has fascinated foreign friends and baffled girlfriends. It can be the most beautiful thing in the world and the most knuckle-gnawingly frustrating. It is simple – it really is: you hit the ball and run – and yet magnificently, gloriously, stupendously pompous. The Marmite of sports, it inspires love and hatred in equal measure. It is a byword for all kinds of absurd notions and, while apparently being little more than freemasonry in whites, its linguistic tentacles have spread well beyond the boundary. It has given me a career of sorts, yet with every year that passes it seems to take me further away from the possibility of ever doing anything else. Its insignificance infuriates me, then something happens to rekindle the flames.

Allow a reminiscence to make my point. The first game I covered for a national newspaper was Derbyshire v Warwickshire at Derby, a venue which has always tested the cricket lover's faith. It was 12 September 2001, yet here I was, sent to a windswept ground at the end of the season to write 150 words for the *Daily Telegraph* on a day cut short by a gale and attended by a few old blokes in flat caps and raincoats. The old joke about county cricket's core audience being three men and a dog sprang to mind when one of the local journalists pointed out that Derbyshire were selling cut-price memberships that year to . . . dogs. And, blow me if there, not fifteen yards in front of the press box, wasn't one of the little creatures wandering around on a lead held by a county official, utterly oblivious to the intricacies of Charlie Dagnall's outswing (the dog, not the official, although who can say for sure?). And then it struck me: even on the day after global politics had taken a tragic twist, it was felt that people were still interested enough in the soothing quirks and rhythms of the county game for a reporter to be sent to cover a game in the second division of the championship.

What *was* this thing called cricket? Escapism? Maybe. Confirmation of an eternal verity? Possibly. A reassuring slice of Englishness? Almost certainly. Thus, in a piece in next day's *Telegraph* headlined 'Derbyshire in doghouse', the final paragraph concluded with an indulgent nod to the comforting weirdness of it all: 'Dogs have had to pay

£2 to gain admission here this summer but only one bothered to turn up. It was not hard to see why.' My experience at Derby could have tricked me into thinking no one cared. Yet in a strange way lots of people quite clearly do (and the international bias of this book reflects the fact that the overwhelming majority of them do not live in a place ending in 'shire'). Here was a cosy world watched in the flesh by not very many people at all yet followed in the posher papers and on the internet by tens of thousands who mind very much that Gloucestershire are 200 for four at tea and that Hampshire have just avoided the follow-on.

Do these people care too much? Who am I, an inveterate neck-craner, to say? It's not a question that can be answered in a hurry, which is probably why I decided to write a leisurely book that finds space for the two distinct cricket people eyeballing each other within me: the not-too-serious fan and the occasionally more serious journalist, and often the other way round. More than anything, this book is an attempt to get to grips with a world that has taken up far too much of my time since I first caught the bug twenty years ago. Where better to start than by examining the people who made me catch it . . .

The Players

IF CRICKET encourages you to be Peter Pan, then occasionally Captain Hook wades in to deliver what sportsmen refer to as a wake-up call. Before you know it, the wake-up call has become a learning curve, and a steep one at that. And so it was with me. Until the age of 23, I laboured under the impression that international cricketers were cut from a different cloth. I was convinced happiness was an Ashes century at Lord's, with 98 of the runs coming off Glenn McGrath. And I would have thrown down the gauntlet to anyone who thought that a cover-drive off Curtly Ambrose was anything less than a gift from the gods. Actually, I still believe these things. But for me the idea that cricketers inhabit a more elevated plane than the rest of us was once tested to the limit.

Rewind to June 1998. I was nearing the end of my university finals, where I had been preparing for my career as a cricket journalist by writing essays on the likes of Goethe (the archetypal all-rounder: clearly Weimar's answer to David Capel), and Voltaire (who might not have agreed with the concept of cricket but would surely have defended our right to play it). Out of the blue an opportunity cropped up that I had spent my formative years dreaming about: I had the chance to meet one of my cricket heroes (his identity must remain a secret I take with me to the grave, unless someone pays me enough to escape to a safe house). He and his wife would be spending the weekend with friends of friends, and would I like to head to a secret location in the north of England to assail him with a breakdown of his career stats? The offer might have been phrased slightly differently, but that wasn't the point. It was like asking me whether Tony Blair was Catholic or Essex played once a year at Southend-on-Sea. Hell, I would always have a degree that would prove little or no use outside France, Germany and Luxembourg. But I might never get another chance to breathe in the same air as a man whose every run for England sent me into paroxysms of pleasure (sex was still a relatively recent discovery). Give me a moment to prepare my pie charts, I shrieked, and I'll be there.

By the time the last dregs had been drained that fateful evening, my hero had fallen so far from his pedestal that Satan's plunge to hell looked like a mishap with a small stepladder. Reeling drunk after being plied with booze to reward him for looking after the barbecue in the drizzle and for humouring my ravings, he had done the following: tried it on with my girlfriend at the dinner table, despite the fact I was sitting on the other side of her and had already regaled him for free with my impression of Michael Holding; exposed a skimpy black thong (even Peter Stringfellow might have drawn the line at that one); and told my girlfriend's mother that she had better keep an eye on her other daughter because she would be 'out shagging in [name of town deleted] tonight'. To crown it all, he had declared with no thought whatsoever for my feelings that there was more to life than scoring a hundred at Lord's.

Before I could scream 'some of us would give our right hand and more to score a hundred at Lord's, you bastard', my hero's wife, determined to get in on the act, was propositioning me with a 'barbecue in [name of town deleted]'.

I had arrived hoping to get to grips with the mind of a man whose fortunes I had followed with bewildering dedication. I left fighting off fantasies of middle-aged swingers. 'Every hero becomes a bore at last,' wrote the American philosopher and poet Ralph Waldo Emerson. For me, the process took a few hours.

Our paths didn't cross much after that, although I did once try to reach him via his wife for a piece I was writing. It took her a while to work out who I was ('I was very drunk that night'), but she did give me her husband's mobile number and promised to let him know I would be calling. When – heart pounding – I tried it, his phone was switched off. On another occasion, a magazine asked me to interview him. As a freelancer, I would probably have danced naked around Leicester if it meant another cheque in the post. But I said no. I would have felt grubby. And besides, the chances were he would have exclusively revealed that the boys had given 110 per cent and that tomorrow was another day.

Most people react to this story with a sympathetic smile and a smug reference to some smart-arse who once said you should never meet your hero because he might try it on with your girlfriend and fail to laugh at your Michael Holding impression. Yet I wouldn't have missed my brush with four-in-a-bed suburbia for anything. After all, it taught me a lesson I have not forgotten. Strip away their abnormally good hand–eye coordination, and cricketers are not a million miles away from you and me. They get drunk, flirt with as many people as they can possibly get away with, and wear skimpy black thongs. Granted, it was not entirely necessary to advertise the underwear, but then who reading this can honestly say they've never flashed their pants while under the influence? And besides, I think I might occasionally let my hair down if I had to meet people like, well, a 23-year-old version of me on a regular basis.

I was once having a quiet beer in a bar in the sleepy New Zealand town of Napier when three England players, all future captains, sat down at a nearby table. Before they could order a drink, a well-heeled, middle-aged Englishman walked over, barked 'Evening, boys', plonked a champagne flute in front of each of them, filled them to the brim and called over his wife to take a photo of the happy foursome. Then he disappeared, leaving the bemused players with glasses of cheap fizz they probably didn't want on the eve of a one-day international and, I imagined, the sense that they had just provided the rather lame material for a story that would be dined out on for the rest of their assailant's life. And this was the behaviour of a bloke at least twice my age. No wonder cricketers like to let it all hang out from time to time. It's the idea that they should let it all hang *in* which messes everything up in the first place.

So when people wonder what cricketers are really like, I usually begin with the black-thong anecdote. It does the job at a harmless-seaside-smut level and I can see now that, in a mildly unnerving kind of way, it actually humanises cricketers more than I realised. And once I've got that story out of the way, I proceed to threaten those who are still awake with several more. Eventually, they plead dinner with their next-door neighbour and leave in a hurry, but not before I have laid out my Defining Characteristics of the Average Modern Cricketer . . .

- Athletic. There are exceptions, of course, and any contemporary cricketer who flaunts his pints or fags is usually deemed to be a 'member of the old school': think Darren Lehmann or Jimmy Ormond. But most of them are broad-shouldered, lithe-limbed and the best part of six foot. The sods.
- Good-looking. Annoyingly so. But really, find your own girlfriends.
- Blessed with a certain amount of self-regard – the kind that nestles between confidence and arrogance and which cannot quite understand why women aren't impressed by the concept of 1000 runs before the end of May.
- Right of centre when pushed on the question of politics. Things have calmed down since Arthur Gilligan, who captained England in the 1920s, enrolled with the British Union of Fascists, although John Arlott used to reckon there were fewer than half a dozen non-Tory voters in the county game.
- Reasonably bright. There are exceptions. Darren Gough once told his England team-mates that he had spent the previous evening at an Italian restaurant called Albarone (All Bar One to you and me), although it is unclear whether Jacques Kallis really did ask a South African team-mate how far above sea level they were as they jogged along a beach in Sri Lanka.
- Surprisingly thin-skinned. Gough and Kallis are probably consulting their lawyers as you read this.
- Up for a laugh. In other words, they will probably try to sleep with anything in a skirt, including Scotsmen.
- Generally a good bunch, which I have just added because of a guilty conscience about most of the above.

Other than that, cricketers preclude the pigeonhole. But it's fun trying to squeeze them in there.

The truth is that the average cricket team is remarkable for its sheer variety of wildlife. In 2007, the *Daily Telegraph* produced a supplement called 'Second Innings'. As if to demonstrate the sport's eclecticism, it looked at '100 Amazing Lives After Cricket' and listed a few of them on its front cover: 'Actor, Dancer, Poet, Monk, Prime Minister, Painter, Policeman, Pilot, Boxer, Opera Singer, Chicken Farmer, Jockey, Wimbledon Champion, Doctor, Author, All Black, Game Hunter, Mountaineer, Dentist, Glass Blower, Bishop.' In football, such non-conformity would be frowned upon. A player who reads, say, the *Guardian*, like Graeme le Saux, is called a homosexual, not just by the fans but by one or two of his peers as well. In cricket, each national paper probably has a reader in every side. After England's decisive win at Headingley over South Africa in 1998, a young Andrew Flintoff was captured in the dressing room studying the less intellectual pages of the *Daily Star*. By contrast, Phil Edmonds, the former Middlesex left-arm spinner and now a business-man, used to flick through the *Financial Times* and dash off to his nearby offices during breaks for rain at Lord's. As his biographer Simon Barnes wrote: 'The only reason he was in a team was so that he could be different from everybody else.'

Bowling off-breaks at the other end from Edmonds was John Emburey, whose expletive-laden explanation of a back injury long ago entered cricketing and medical folklore. Peas from different pods, these were men united only by their desire to bowl the perfect arm-ball and go for less than two runs an over. For in what other sport could the same side include one player with a double first in history from Cambridge and another who once described his hobby thus: 'We ran the bulls down in an old Land Cruiser with the tyres on the front. We knocked them over and tied them up and whacked them in the back of what we call a lion cage and carted them off to the markets. It was great fun.' For some reason, Ed Smith and Andrew Symonds never quite saw eye to eye on the game's finer points.

Vive la différence might not be the most obvious motto for this English-speaking game, but several cricketers would be able to pronounce it, and a decent number could tell you where to place the acute accent. This is a sport where, by and large, university degrees are not regarded as evidence of a misspent youth. In fact, it is a sport where one of the less demanding university degrees could probably be acquired over the course of a season during the lunch interval. It even used to be a prerequisite for the England captain to have studied Ancient History at Oxford or Land Economy at Cambridge. Mike Brearley went one better and came top of the civil-service exams, later turning his 'degree in people' (copyright: Rodney Hogg) into a job as a psychoanalyst. The Nottinghamshire seamer A.J. Harris revealed that he spent time recovering from an injury by reading Jed Rubenfeld's *The Interpretation of Murder*, which – as he casually put it – 'touches on Freud and Jung'. Andrew Strauss has been known to conclude his *Sunday Telegraph* column by quoting Friedrich Nietzsche, who would surely have made a thoughtful but wild fast bowler with an unpredictable line in put-downs. John Snow, a thoughtful but wild fast bowler with an unpredictable line in put-downs, wrote poetry, as did Frank Tyson, even wilder and faster but also a schoolteacher when he wasn't terrorising batsmen, and said to recite Wordsworth on the way back to his mark. 'I like what you write, Frank,' the Australian wicketkeeper Barry Jarman once said of Tyson's scribblings. 'But why use all those long words? Don't forget us readers who only had a technical education. I only understand three long words – wheelbarrow, minestrone and mulligatawny.'

But then that was one of the things I always enjoyed about playing cricket at university: the fact it attracted such a wide social mix. If the college footballers were the athletes and the womanisers, the rugby players were the drinkers and the womanisers, and the pool players were the inveterate gamblers and the maths students, the cricketers were often those who proved incompetent at everything else. In one or two cases, they were incompetent at cricket too. Yet it was that promise of a glimpse of a soupçon of a moment in the sun that persuaded some of the flabbier minds of Sidney Sussex College to waste whole summer afternoons getting thrashed by bigger, better Cambridge institutions. One team-mate, known to all as Grim – yes, he came from the north – was particularly hopeless. His all-round ability back then could be likened to that of Devon Malcolm, but without the raw pace or prowess with the bat. Then, in a game against Fitzwilliam College, Grim suddenly clicked. Batting first, Sidney Sussex crumpled to 90 for nine (Booth yorked for nine) when Grim shuffled out to the middle. Something about his shambling gait persuaded the Fitzwilliam captain to bring back his opening bowler (4–3–4–2), at which point, to the utter astonishment of his team-mates, Grim scythed five successive off-side fours. He wasn't finished. Fitzwilliam had reached about 50 for three in pursuit of 115 or so when the Sidney captain tossed the ball in Grim's direction. You guessed it: three wickets in an over, followed by a diving catch at midwicket moments later. Not a word of a lie! Naturally, Grim never played cricket again. We all knew he could never reproduce those heroics, and I think he knew it himself. I also doubt whether any other sport could have furnished him with the opportunity to taste such fleeting and utterly misleading glory.

Now, I don't want to get all high-minded about the kind of people cricket attracts, but it's surely no coincidence that England's players once revealed their collective nous by appearing on a special edition of *The Weakest Link*, even if the effect was only marginally spoiled by Matthew Hoggard. Asked by Anne Robinson, 'In which film did Harry Lime say: "In Switzerland they had brotherly love, they had five hundred years of democracy and peace, and what did that produce? The cuckoo clock"?' he replied: '*One Flew Over the Cuckoo Clock*'. If nothing else, that backed up the view expressed by Phil Edmonds's wife, Frances, who accompanied her husband on England's hideous tour of the Caribbean in 1985–86: 'Nowhere is it easier to pass muster as an intellectual than on the professional cricket circuit,' she later wrote. 'In the land of CSE, he with the GCE rules.' But then Frances Edmonds was very bright, and acerbic with it. And in general naivety is laughed at: Pakistan's Abdul Razzaq could not understand why he came down with a bout of vomiting, dizziness and breathing difficulties during a Test in Melbourne, until it was pointed out that all he ever ate was spinach.

One inevitable corollary of making reasonably intelligent young men hang around for four or five days to play a game they might only be involved in for half the time is the scope for pranks. For reasons known only to the cricketers themselves, sock-snipping is a favourite. The former Glamorgan and two-time England opener Steve James once received one of his socks in the post cut in five pieces after he failed to heed a letter warning him to wear his sweatshirt round his waist during training. But when his county colleague and habitual japester Robert Croft cut the ends off the socks belonging to the future England coach Duncan Fletcher, then hung around to watch him pull them halfway up his leg, Fletcher flipped. 'He was seething,' wrote James in his autobiography. 'And I had to drive him home!' In a game so reliant on bats, balls and other paraphernalia, it is perhaps no surprise that props figure so highly in cricketing jokes. Derek Randall once walked out to bat only to discover that his gloves had been stuffed with condoms by Ian Botham and Allan Lamb, England's high priests of slapstick in the 1980s. And Botham was still at it a couple of decades later in the Sky commentary box: when Nasser Hussain took off his shoes in preparation for a nap, Botham tied the laces together and shoved them in a freezer.

And so it goes on. Dickie Bird – our one celebrity umpire – has managed to fill at least twenty-seven auto-biographies with the story of the time he found a rubber snake in his pocket, courtesy of Dennis Lillee, and mistook it for a real one (so real, in fact, that when the serpent reappeared later in Dickie's lunchtime soup, he was traumatised all over again). But not half as traumatised as readers of the 2000 edition of *Wisden Cricketers' Almanack*. Take a look, if you dare, at page 657, where you will find the Leicestershire team photo. Then look at Matt Brimson, standing fourth from the left in the middle row.

Then look at his crotch. Yes, Brimson's manhood was possibly the first ever to appear in the holiest of cricket publications, leading to cries of 'What a knob' at county-cricket club bars throughout the land. Reassuringly, Brimson later left the game to become a teacher. Oh, and if you don't know the one about Andrew Flintoff dipping his freshly bruised testicles into a pint of iced water moments before his Lancashire team-mate Gary Yates walked in gasping for a drink, then you really need to get out less.

I sometimes wonder if this is what the players mean when they talk about dressing-room camaraderie. Does a retired cricketer really yearn for the joys of emptying a cellar of salt all over his lunch because a tittering team-mate loosened the screw top seconds earlier? Does he weep tears of nostalgia when his wife forgets to nail the bag containing his gym kit to the living-room floor? Do his shoulders slump in disappointment when the socks he puts on every morning fail to have a hole in them? The answer, if Nasser Hussain's deep-frozen shoes are anything to go by, does not need spelling out.

With all the merriment going on, it is surprising just how touchy some players can be. Now, I am happy to admit that there is more than an element of the pot calling the kettle black here. If a journalist writes a book and gets a glowing review that contains the line 'but not quite as jaw-droppingly erudite and wet-my-pants funny as his first publication', he will flounce around for a week while plotting his revenge on the reviewer who was a) probably the best man at his wedding, and b) under the illusion that he had done his mate a favour by giving the book a five-star rating and calling it an 'all-time classic'. Even though he hadn't got round to reading it. Yet for sheer sensitivity, cricketers take some beating.

I'm not thinking here of the number of doors, windows and assorted thresholds destroyed by Australian openers over the years. No, I'm thinking of the red mist that descends on otherwise reasonable men when someone has the nerve to take a pop at their technique against the short, rising, 95 mph brute of a ball directed straight at the head. The effect is multiplied if the critic is someone whose idea of testing conditions is Uncle Len bowling underarm in the back garden and who has gone straight from the student union bar to the press box, missing out that whole first-class-career business in the middle. Someone, then, like me. As Marcus Trescothick once said while a whole generation of non-ex-playing journalists hung their heads in shame: 'The only people worth listening to are those who played the game.'

Is this really the case? One evening during the 2006–07 Ashes I found myself at a cheap and cheerful Adelaide eatery talking to a local journalist and a member of the Australian back-room staff. The subject of Brett Lee's bowling in the first Test at Brisbane cropped up and my colleague and I agreed that a match analysis of two for 149 was nothing to write home about. 'Couldn't hit a barn door with a beamer,' we chuckled as we smugly shovelled in another forkful of carbonara. Then the Australian insider told us a short story. Sitting around in the dressing room after Australia's pummelling victory, their wicket-keeper Adam Gilchrist had remarked to Lee how he had never seen him bowl so well. Bah, we scoffed, swigging another mouthful of Chianti: that's just one team-mate building up the confidence of another. Au contraire, countered the insider: the stats had shown that Gilchrist had not needed to take a single one of Lee's deliveries down the leg-side. He had bowled 37 overs in all. There was only one possible conclusion to draw from this shock revelation: what in the name of Shane Warne did *we* know?

On another occasion, I was covering a county game at Old Trafford between Lancashire and Surrey. Several Surrey batsmen had thrown away their wickets on the first morning of the game. Or so it seemed to me. So when their coach, Keith Medlycott, wandered up to the press box, which, unlike the Old Trafford dressing rooms, provides a view from behind the bowler's arm, I ambled over in search of a quote. The response could not have returned me to my hovel more expertly than if Medlycott had picked me up by the lapels and placed me there himself. 'History tells you that batsmen tend to get out,' he explained, just about managing to stay on the civil side of the line that divides tolerance from disdain. It was difficult to argue with. But, hey, if the Lord God Almighty had a glaring weakness against the ball that jags in late off the seam, then journos would need to risk eternal damnation by pointing it out.

If it really is true that the intricacies of cricket are decipherable only by those who have played the game at the highest level, where does that leave the rest of us? And who, in that case, are the players playing for? Why bother playing at all? The answer in the most extreme instances is that they are playing for the bubble, the imaginary film that protects a team from malevolent intruders, commonly known as everyone else. The trouble is that the bubble can only work for so long before the outside world reasserts itself, usually in the form of pesky journalists who are pushed further and further into the realms of speculation the more they are given the cold shoulder. Who benefits? Not the players, who end up declaring that any vaguely harrowing incident beyond the bubble gives them 'perspective'. And not the public, who are kept at arm's length even while the tickets for which they fork out pay the players' wages. The genuine bemusement in the Australian dressing room when their behaviour during the tempestuous 2007–08 series against India was criticised by the Australian public shows just how illusory the bubble can be – and the Aussies are among the more fan-friendly sides. It might come as no surprise to learn that, in terms of press–player relations, I much prefer Mike Gatting's view. Asked after he had captained England to Ashes glory in 1986–87 whether he felt 'the selectors and yourself have been vindicated by the result', he replied: 'I don't think the press are vindictive. They can write what they want.'

Still, at least the players can't accuse journalists like me of being turncoats. Their attitude to ex-players-turned-hacks, though, is another matter. I once covered an Indian tour of New Zealand, where Martin Crowe had made the transition from rapier-like batsman to cutting TV commentator. At the time, he had been getting stuck into Sourav Ganguly. It is fair to say that Ganguly, then India's captain, has not always been everyone's cup of chai. Indeed his personal skills were so unorthodox that after making a half-century for Lancashire, he turned round to acknowledge his team-mates' applause on the balcony to find no one was there. Needless to say, Ganguly did not like the cut of Crowe's jib and immediately broke two golden rules. One, never indulge the press by saying nasty things about someone else which will only sound nastier once they have been through the hands of a journalist and a sub-editor.

Two – and this one is close to my heart – never stand accused of being a sad anorak who knows too many obscure stats for his own good. 'It is natural that when a team loses, the captain will come in for a lot of criticism,' began Ganguly, preparing himself for a triumphant punchline. 'But definitely not from one who won just two of his sixteen Tests as captain – a win record of 12 per cent – when compared to someone with a win record of 40 per cent.' Don't you just love the catty precision? Presumably Crowe's response ('Yes, he was right about me winning two Tests out of sixteen, but remember when I started we hardly had any bowling worth the name') did not go down well with his former team-mates.

Yes, cricketers are a competitive lot, all right. Because for all the cant and blather about cricket being a team game, which club player would – hand on heart – rather be run out without facing a ball in a game his side ends up winning than score a heroic, average-fattening hundred in defeat? The answer, mercifully, is that such sanctimony does not exist, except when you are talking to professionals who don't want to stand accused of forgetting time-honoured platitudes such as 'There's no "I" in team'.

Or, as V.S. Naipaul, the cricket-loving novelist from Trinidad, once put it: 'Cricket, a team game? Teams play, and one team is to be willed to victory. But it is the individual who remains in the memory, he who has purged the emotions by delight and fear.' The references to 1981 as 'Botham's Ashes' suggest he has a point.

Cricketers want to win at everything, as the epic PlayStation battles over the years between Michael Vaughan and Ashley Giles used to demonstrate. They even want to win at, well, not winning. 'I'm never, ever, going to succumb to the PlayStation,' seethed Nasser Hussain, possibly after being strapped to a chair and forced to watch Vaughan and Giles battle it out on Brian Lara's Cricket. The Australians, who would stage World Championship Staring Matches if – God forbid – they ever found themselves locked in a dungeon in the middle of the desert, even divided their dressing room into Nerds and Julios just for the competitive thrill of it. The Nerds were characters like Glenn McGrath, who would trim the overhanging edges off his fried egg on toast and bowled with an off-centre parting. The Julios were men like Damien Martyn, who was too busy perfecting the just-got-up look to bother with troublesome egg white and had such a high regard for his own image that he was accused by his former fiancée of leaving Post-it notes around the house signed 'Love, Becks'.

I have myself experienced the competitive irrepressibility of the international cricketer at first hand. I should start by saying that Andrew Flintoff is a lovely man. The sports psychologist Jamie Edwards, who imbued Flintoff with confidence after the first Test against Australia at Lord's in 2005, said at the time, 'I've never met somebody of his standing who is so humble,' which pretty well sums him up. But on at least two occasions, Flintoff has left me a little the worse for wear. Should his team-mates complain of being 'Fredded', it refers to a night on the town when they have been unable to knock back the buckets of fizzy lager Flintoff suggests they consume as a quick chaser. My own personal Fredding took place at a colleague's stag do in Wellington, where Flintoff's role was to wander around the dinner table like the grim reaper, tilt back the hacks' heads and – when they had committed some heinous crime, like drinking with their left hand, or using the word 'sensational', a favourite of the groom-to-be – pour great chugs of vodka down their retching throats. I'd like to be able to say that we all had a good laugh afterwards, but things became a little hazy. For all I know, I may have told Flintoff he was a complete waste of space and that I and all my colleagues knew he would never make anything of himself. No one has since been able to confirm or deny this.

Which might explain what happened the next time our paths crossed outside the confines of the press-conference charade. After no persuasion whatsoever, I had agreed to face an over each from Flintoff and the Gloucestershire and England seamer Jon Lewis in the indoor nets at Lord's for a piece in *Men's Health* magazine. On my previous trip to the nets, I had made one of my dinky medium-pacers swing towards leg before nipping back to beat the outside edge of my startled mate's bat. It was my very own ball of the century. I still treasure the memory. But if a 5 ft 9 in, 50 mph trundler could manage that much, what would Lewis and Flintoff do? Humming loudly to myself to block out negative thoughts, I stuttered towards the metal stumps, resembling the Michelin man's less svelte older brother. Lewis, it turned out, was fine. I had written a complimentary piece about him the week before, which he remembered – this remains the only article a player has ever told me he liked – and he proceeded to bowl off a few paces. Hey, I was even enjoying myself. Then along came Fred. My mind began to work overtime. Had I ever libelled him? Did he take that line about puppy fat the wrong way? What if he felt he had gone too easy on the vodka that night in Wellington? My musings were interrupted by a small red blur heading straight for my unprotected ribs. It is to my everlasting relief that I dug it out at the last moment. Two deliveries wide of off-stump followed – rarely have cut shots made more definitive contact with fresh air – before, well, let's call it the moment of truth.

Freddie, it turned out, was getting bored. I know this because Mark, one of the PR people who had arranged the net session, was standing near the top of Freddie's run-up and heard him say, 'I'm bored.' Actually, Mark hadn't been standing near the top of Freddie's run-up until then. Until then, he had been standing at the far end of the hall, but Andrew 'I'm bored' Flintoff had extended his run-up so far that his world-weary, *sotto voce* utterance had been all too audible. Looking back, it was quite clear that Freddie charged in with the kind of murderous intent he would later reserve for Ricky Ponting in *that* over at Edgbaston, where he seemed to fit five lbw appeals and six lethal leg-cutters into the space of a few deliveries. Mark even claimed he could see the pupils in Freddie's eyes dilate with excitement. I was spared the preliminaries: the ball was fast, short of a length, straight at my head and might well have killed me had I not got my left wrist in the way. I ask for no sympathy. The ball ricocheted over my head and away for four runs, which I only marginally resisted the temptation to signal by going down on one knee and flourishing my one remaining good arm like Tony Greig used to do to Dennis Lillee. 'You all right?' enquired Flintoff. 'Is that the best you've got, you overrated nancy?' I replied. Or at least I would have done if I hadn't been too busy noticing that Mark and the other journalists waiting to come face-to-face with this hulking juggernaut suddenly looked like Jack Nicholson's Joker in *Batman*, but without the grin. As I passed Freddie on the way out of the nets, I asked him how much effort he had put in. 'Sixty per cent,' he said. 'Maybe fifty.' I made a mental note never to criticise a tail-ender for backing away against a fast bowler. Ever. Again.

I don't think Flintoff wanted to hurt me. I just think it was a combination of being unable to do anything for any length of time at less than full tilt, and of not having the faintest idea of his own strength. Shortly afterwards, we had to pose for a photo which involved him holding my helmeted head in a neck-lock and staring menacingly into the camera. It's fair to say he almost strangled me and was none the wiser.

Perhaps being around international cricketers the whole time had given Flintoff an unrealistic image of everyone else, just as hanging around with cricket writers leads you to wonder why the rest of the world is incapable of surviving on a steady diet of liquid lunches. When cricket journalists want to reassure themselves that they are in fact far more rounded than the bat-wielders and ball-slingers they write about, they make sniffy allusions to a player's hinterland, damning him with faint praise by accusing him of reading the *Daily Sport* or, worse, *The Da Vinci Code*. Shane Warne once provided ample ammunition for the snobs when he turned up for an interview with an Australian journalist who had been passing the time by reading a book. 'I read this book once,' said Warne. 'It was about U.F.O.s.'

Having already argued that cricketers are on average brighter than most sportsmen, I need to be careful how I go here. I think it's probably the case that, like plenty of people in other walks of life, some of them can't be bothered to apply their minds outside their own profession, with the result that they get bored very easily when faced with the need to adapt. On a tour of Sri Lanka a few years ago, the New Zealand players went so far as to demand a change of hotel in Dambulla because the one they were staying in was short of sports channels. Climbing the Rock of Sigiriya to soak up the stunning scenery clearly wasn't enough. I was also struck by the grumbles of the English tourists in Pakistan in 2005–06. They had left Heathrow extolling the team-bonding virtues of staying in a country where the nightlife meant long evenings together in the hotel, but ended up complaining of claustrophobia and boredom. They would have been better off admitting that they were fed up with losing. But usually travelling cricketers very quickly discover their own ways to entertain themselves, though not all the activities would find pride of place on the postcards home. Some, though, are more upfront than others: for sheer shock value nothing can compare with the question reportedly posed by a West Indies player to the cricket official who was engaging him in rather too earnest conversation at some function or other. Turning to his tormentor, he asked: 'You get much pussy?'

Being cool may come easily to such players, who probably only take off their shades in the shower, but it does not come easily to most cricketers, and nor should it. Standing around for several days in the field playing a game that, according to most reputable surveys, 43 per cent of Britain's under-25s believe is less appealing than a hairy wart just isn't particularly fashionable these days. Most players accept this. Matthew Hoggard relaxes by walking his dogs on the Yorkshire Dales and is happy to admit as much. The Hampshire seamer Billy Taylor is a tree surgeon. Graham Thorpe used to fiddle with bat handles, which is the kind of geekiness only cricket would tolerate. And when the players try to stray out of a world in which the names of many of the domestic teams sound like settings in a Jane Austen novel, they often end up looking like football wannabes. Kevin Pietersen is one of the best things to happen to English cricket for years and I love watching him bat, but his efforts to position himself for a crack at *I'm A Celebrity* . . . have been undermined in hilarious fashion at almost every turn. Take the haircut he was sporting when he trounced Australia at The Oval in 2005. Now, Pietersen really did think it was cool. But Ian Botham said it reminded him of a dead mongoose and I'm with him. Even Kevin's own mum may have had her doubts. 'No matter what happens,' said Penny Pietersen, 'a mother will always love her son.' She might as well have dragged Kevin by the ear from the crease for all the good her comments did his street cred. Perhaps the crowning iconoclastic glory came when a kiss-'n'-tell luvvly alleged in the *News of the World* that Pietersen insisted she shout his name at the crucial moment. It's hard to look a man square in the eye after that.

And yet sex is inescapable, which may not surprise those who genuinely think 'googly' is a rude word and snigger every time it crops up in polite conversation. With a few eye-watering exceptions, cricketers tend not to go in for the footballer's staple diet of dogging and roasting, although a former England international did remark to me that one of his old room-mates on tour was not the sort to 'help you out with a threesome'. That isn't to say that appetites are not on the voracious side of healthy. A female journalist posing as a groupie at the 2002 ICC Champions

Trophy in Colombo, where on a dark night you will encounter all sorts of women in the foyers of the posher hotels, claimed that one fast bowler 'was all ours post-match, if we wanted him'. She could have been writing about practically any cricketer in the hotel, married or engaged, divorced or single, and probably even gay. To become one of the boys it helps to prove your prowess in the pulling stakes. 'I'm crap at talking to girls,' claimed the fresh-faced England fast bowler Jimmy Anderson when he first arrived in international cricket. 'I really need them to come and chat to me, but I'm learning a lot from the England guys.' A couple of years later he tied the knot with a former Miss UK, who had obviously not read Derek Pringle's article in the 2003 *Wisden* entitled 'Don't Marry a Cricketer'. Pringle – a bachelor himself – put it thus: 'Fame has always been a potent aphrodisiac,' even if that fails to explain why unknown county cricketers always seem to fancy their chances on trips to towns like Colchester and Scarborough.

But if there's one thing worse than not being seen to cut a swathe through the fleshpots of the game's outposts, it is to be accused of – nudge, wink – batting for the other side. In the women's game this is not an issue. But among the men even the slightest whisper can spark a Richard Gere/Cindy Crawford-style public denial. The Australian openers Justin Langer and Matthew Hayden were more tactile than most at the crease, mainly because they were so busy bear-hugging each other after their latest double-century partnership. But when observers began to look at them askance, Langer took decisive action. 'It's uncommon to see two men show such emotion to each other in a public arena,' he wrote in his autobiography, 'and questions have been asked about our sexuality. I can report that neither of us is homosexual.'

In general, I have always found cricketers a good-natured lot. A little self-absorbed at times, and with a tendency to talk in clichés, perhaps, but as a bunch I rather like them. I'm well aware that not everyone shares my view. Wasim Bari, Pakistan's former chairman of selectors, once said of India's Rahul Dravid, one of the game's genuinely good guys, 'I found him a decent person, unlike normal cricketers.' I wondered who he had in mind. To me, normal cricketers are pretty much normal people. And if you reckon you wouldn't have waded into the crowd with a bat to deal with a heckler who was calling you a potato through a megaphone, then you're obviously a better person than Inzamam-ul-Haq. Although, as I hope the next chapter shows, I am not suggesting this is the kind of behaviour you should necessarily expect from a Pakistani cricketer. Stereotypes, as we all know, have no place in an increasingly cosmopolitan world . . .

2

THE TEAMS

A ND YET stereotypes in cricket, like a Shaun Pollock bouncer, are sometimes hard to avoid. I was once chatting with an Australian friend about the laziness of such cheap and gratuitous characterisation. Bruce responded with a grunt last heard in the Triassic Period, then returned to his bottle of VB lager and his game of Flick the Dangling Corks. He amused himself this way for several hours before collapsing in a drunken heap and burbling away in the corner about the baggy green.

Of course, the above paragraph contains elements of fiction (Bruce's name was actually Shane). The sad truth is that my various friendships with Australians only just survived the ritual slaughter that took place between 1989 and 2003. In that time the English were stereotyped to the point where they could barely dunk their custard creams in their Earl Greys without provoking a snort of derision from the Antipodes: dirty, spineless, useless; ridiculous, ineffectual, embarrassing; lily-livered, weak-hearted, pasty-faced. But it was when the Aussies started to get personal that reality dawned. Cricket is not merely a feeble pretext for nationalistic gloating in and around the pubs of south-west London. More than that, it is a great excuse for getting to grips with what makes a country tick; for exposing foibles and laughing at them; and for wondering, deep down, whether the caricatures we all rely on to make life simpler do not in fact have their basis in that scary place which, as we have already discussed, many cricketers try to avoid: the real world.

It is true that generalisations are particular fodder for journalists (you know, those boozy layabouts who doctor their quotes and would happily denounce their own grandmothers in print if it paid for the next round). Pigeonholes, after all, make for more straightforward judgements. We love batsmen like Ken Barrington, who in the words of Australia's great post-war wicketkeeper Wally Grout used to approach the crease with the Union Jack 'trailing behind him'. And we love them because we know where we stand. We feel unsettled when a Welshman who was born in Papua New Guinea but grew up in Australia keeps wicket for England, because we don't know who to blame when things go wrong. In fact, it's simple: he's British when he takes a catch, Australian when he doesn't, and Papuan when the editor demands a fluffy feature on a quiet news day. These days, with Geraint Jones no longer in the side, it's even simpler.

It is the kind of childish thinking which means that each of the Test nations is invariably ascribed its own set of characteristics, especially when a deadline is approaching. Australians never say die, unless they are standing on the throat of a Pom who hasn't showered for a week. New Zealanders are understated and have an inferiority complex about Australians. South Africans are humourless and competitive. Indians are wristy. Pakistanis are mercurial, if not downright excitable. West Indians used to be frightening; now they are simply too cool for their own good. Sri Lankans are joyful islanders, despite the civil war that has engulfed their country (note the patronising caveat: this is something of a rule of thumb too). Bangladeshis are plucky, except if they beat Australia, when they become demi-Gods. Zimbabweans are hapless. And the English?

33

That's a tricky one. The English, more than any other nation, are the sum of their parts, and those parts can be very disparate indeed. During England's disastrous one-day tour of India in 2006, their top six contained Andrew Strauss, Matt Prior (both born in Johannesburg), Owais Shah (Karachi), Kevin Pietersen (Pietermaritzburg) and Vikram Solanki (Udaipur, India). Geraint Jones (the Australian-born, Papua New Guinean-bred Welshman) came in at No. 7. It all made Paul Collingwood (Shotley Bridge), Andrew Flintoff (Preston), Ian Blackwell (Chesterfield) and Liam Plunkett (Middlesbrough) sound distinctly one-dimensional. Of course, this isn't the case. But then stereotypes only work up to a certain point. And this, nation by nation, is my attempt to get to grips with them.

Australia

The Australian prime minister John Howard once described the ideal outlook of any immigrant to his country: he should believe in the principle of equality, the ethic of mateship and the willingness to 'have a go'. Well, blow me down. At least if Howard had shouted the odds for inequality, the ethic of hostility and the willingness to disengage and crack open a tinnie at the slightest pretext, we would have had a decent headline on our hands. Yet there is something amid his banalities that strikes a chord with the average Australian cricketer. Many people believe that Australians regard cricket as a matter of life or death. They do not. And neither do they subscribe to the equivalent of Bill Shankly's observation about football being more important than that. After all, why would you bat like Matthew Hayden or bowl like Brett Lee if you were worried that a single mistake would mean a one-way ticket to the great billabong in the sky?

No, what marks the Aussie cricketer out is his competitive instinct and his genuine disgust at the idea that anyone could ever bat or bowl for a draw, which might explain why all pre-war Ashes Tests down under had to be played to a finish. 'We could be playing Kick a Cockroach From Here to the Wall and we'd want to be competitive,' said Hayden. And he wasn't joking: Sydney airport is full of cockroaches desperate to get out. In Australia, the draw is the refuge of the coward, a relic of English village games where the less talented team can stonewall for three hours and emerge with a share of the spoils. When Matthew Hoggard told the media on the eve of the second Ashes Test at Adelaide in December 2006 that England's aim was 'not to lose', he might as well have donned a Harlequin cap and revealed to horrified Australian journalists that he was the long-lost grandson of Douglas Jardine. And when England spent the last day of that Test, a game they had dominated, trying to do precisely as Hoggard had suggested, they failed spectacularly. For the Australians, it was the only conclusion that made sense.

Like most Englishmen of a certain age, I have developed an irrational problem with Australians. I like them very much on a one-to-one basis, but get them in a group and they begin to grate. And if that group happens to be a cricket team, violence can ensue. The fact that they spent many, many years duffing England up didn't help, although I'll delve into that special relationship later. But what really got me – what really convinced me that green, gold and Skippy were dirty words – was the zealousness with which they went about dismantling England in 2006–07. Everyone likes to beat England: it's one of the perks of being part of a former Empire. But the Aussies define themselves by it. 'Stuff that stiff-upper-lip crap,' snarled the Pom-hater *par excellence* Jeff Thomson. 'Let's see how stiff it is when it's split.' He was talking about bowling bouncers, but no one would have been surprised if he had uttered those words while wiping the beery foam away from his mouth and advancing on a group of 'Rule, Britannia'-singing bystanders. Thomson may have been an extreme case, but not by much. The Aussies love winning. And they love to hate the Poms. The two ingredients make for a potent mix.

If you were to imagine the archetypal Aussie cricketer you would probably grit your teeth and do it something like this. He would have the nerve of the 22-stone Warwick Armstrong, who led his country to a 5–0 victory over England in 1921, and once whiled away the last session of a Test at The Oval by reading a newspaper that had blown across the outfield, 'to see who we're playing against'. He would have the precocity of Neil Harvey, who made his Test debut aged 19 and ended up with twenty-one hundreds, the talented git; the facial hair of Merv Hughes, to muffle the sledging; the fruit-machine-slot eyes of Steve Waugh, dispensing derision and disdain; the verbal dexterity of Matthew Hayden; the harder-than-rusty-nails toughness of Allan Border; the wrist of Shane Warne, although maybe not his texting thumb; the accuracy of Glenn McGrath; the team spirit of Rod Marsh, who in 1984 told Border he was quitting the game 'because my mates have retired'; oh, and the hand–eye coordination of Don Bradman, who according to his team-mates was equally adept off the field, where he never knowingly dug into his own pocket to buy a round. Anyone who has shared an evening's drinking with a bunch of Australians will know this kind of behaviour takes a very special talent indeed.

Much is made of Australia's climate, which has certainly helped encourage fast bowlers, leg-spinners and rabidly keen fielders: the sight of Andrew Symonds tearing up the outfield to turn a three into a two in a game Australia are about to win by an innings is one of the wonders of the age. But the role of geography in Australia's attitude should not be overlooked. Their position on the other side of the world – stop me if I'm getting all GMT-centric – has nurtured their desire to be noticed. All I can say is thank goodness for New Zealand, who have stoically provided a handy bulwark between Australia and the oblivion of Antarctica for many centuries. Without the Kiwis, the Aussies would probably have won the football World Cup too. Throw in the fact that Australian males still toss and turn with resentment every night at the thought of Bodyline and the taunts of the Barmy Army every four years ('God save your gracious Queen' . . . 'Get your six stars off our flag' . . . 'I shagged Matilda, I shagged Matilda') and you get the picture. This is a nation hell-bent on success. I'd say good luck to them, but they hardly need it. And in any case it would be a hideous lie.

Bangladesh

India aside, no Test team has as much potential for improvement as Bangladesh. A country just over half the size of the UK, it contains almost three times as many inhabitants, most of whom are too involved with the day-to-day business of survival to spend their time oiling their bat and polishing the shiny side. And yet it is precisely for this reason that cricket is so important to the Bangladeshis: it is the ultimate means of escape from a reality of flooding and poverty. Those quality-of-life indices that rate nations according to factors such as cost of living, health, infrastructure and the tendency of their terrain to break up and help the spinners on the fourth day regularly place Bangladesh somewhere near the bottom, alongside countries such as Rwanda and Turkmenistan. Now, if 'cricket' really were added as a category . . .

Not everyone is convinced that Bangladesh will make it as a Test-playing nation, which is why most assessments of a player's career tend to include caveats such as 'ignoring for a moment runs made against Zimbabwe and Bangladesh', 'take Bangladesh out of the equation', and 'were it not for his unbeaten triple hundred against the Bangladeshis . . .'. Invited to dine at the top table, the Bangladeshis have generally been asked to sit at the end in the kiddy's chair and are sent to bed before the adults pass the port. This stems in part from a widespread belief that the game which helped them attain Test status in 2000 – their victory over Pakistan at Northampton in the 1999 World Cup – was dodgier than a cut-price deal with Trotters Independent Traders. But I'm not so sure. I mean, the fact that Pakistan bowled twenty-eight wides and seven no-balls and then lost three of their batsmen to farcical run-outs hardly differentiates it from most of their other performances over the years. No matter: Bangladesh, who had never before won a one-day international against a Test-playing nation and would not do so again – Zimbabwe excepted – until Boxing Day 2004, were soon invited to join the club.

It has been a painful apprenticeship, and one which has been alleviated only slightly by the occasional plucky performance against Australia and the comedy value of their press conferences. When most sides lose a game, the local journalists might ask a couple of specific questions. Why was Devon Malcolm batting at No. 3, for example? What possessed Nasser Hussain to open the bowling? Bangladeshi reporters barely bother with such niceties. 'Dav, Dav,' they clamoured, as the former coach Dav Whatmore did his best to hide his irritation. 'Why no bowlers? Why no batsmen?' Then, as he left the room at the end of his grilling, they would swarm round him in search of quotes which had no chance of being exclusive. There have been signs recently that Bangladesh are finally translating potential into results, but I'm happy to say the press conferences are unlikely to become any less frantic.

England

Where better to start with an assessment of the English than through the eyes of a Scot? In *The Angry Island: Hunting the English,* the journalist A.A. Gill (OK, so he doesn't exactly go round in a kilt) wrote: 'An American pointed out that the English are the only people on earth who manage to feel *Schadenfreude* about themselves. There is a long history of self-satisfied masochism in the English, a self-justifying pessimism.' Anyone who grew up following the fortunes of the England cricket team in the 1980s and '90s will be nodding their head right now with vertebra-damaging fury. And while we're getting all Germanic, it seems only fair to mention that these two decades were an era which defined the *Weltanschauung* of an entire generation: defeat was the daily diet, victory an all-too-rare feast. In a twisted kind of way, it was good for the soul, or so I told myself on a self-preservingly regular basis. Just look at the stats. In the 1980s England played 104 Tests, winning 20 and losing 39. In the 1990s they played 107, winning 26 and losing 43. As my old geography teacher used to say after we kept confusing our anticyclones with our depressions: 'Abysmal, gentlemen, abysmal.'

To admit to being an England fan in the days after Ian Botham stopped winning games all by himself was to invite sympathy. But those of us who stuck with them were rewarded: first Nasser Hussain, a very unEnglish kind of Englishman, then Michael Vaughan, who had a touch of Mike Brearley's elegant ruthlessness, turned things round. Suddenly England were beating everyone on a regular basis except Australia, and even they had the good grace to roll over for one series before resuming normal service.

The experience of winning caused a problem, largely because it is not something the English cricketer has been used to over the years. When Mike Atherton accepted a gong on behalf of Channel 4 at the RTS Television Sports Awards in 2006, he could not have phrased his surprise more delicately: 'Before I joined Channel 4 I played for a team that won fuck all for fifteen years.' Success has rarely been part of the national vocabulary. England were the best side in the world until about 1897, when Australia, their only competition, finally got to grips with the game. Their next indisputable period of dominance came in the 1950s, when they had a genuinely world-class side and newcomers like Pakistan, India and New Zealand made them feel even better about themselves. There is also a case for saying they were briefly No. 1 after winning in Australia in 1970–71. But we're getting distracted. The point is that England tend to be at their best when least is expected of them. Some of their most stirring victories in recent times – The Oval 1993, Bridgetown 1994, Adelaide 1995, Melbourne 1998, Mumbai 2006, the XXXX Beach Cricket veterans' tri-series in Perth 2008 – have come when it seemed things could get no worse. Yet slap on them the tag of favourites, and they can hardly walk out of the pavilion without tripping on the steps. When they went to Pakistan in 2005–06 fresh from toppling the Aussies, they came a predictable cropper. As Shane Warne pointed out a year later when Australia took revenge in style, the MBEs they were awarded for winning a couple of games of cricket presumably stood for Must Be Embarrassing. In fact, this very English problem with winning had been summed up a few decades earlier by John Snow, the fast bowler who helped England to victory in that 1970–71 series in Australia. Flying home, he recalls thinking, 'What now?' An Australian who had just beaten England would surely have been thinking, 'When next?'

This natural suspicion of ostentatious glory – to gloss over the Trafalgar Square parade in 2005 for a moment – means the English also manage to find a place in their hearts for players who would not necessarily be considered drawcards elsewhere. While there has always been a rightful helping of reverence for stylish English batsmen down the ages – Frank Woolley, Jack Hobbs, Wally Hammond, Ted Dexter, David Gower – the cult figures in the eyes of England cricket fans have often been the roundheads: Len Hutton, Ken Barrington, Geoff Boycott, Trevor Bailey, Mike Atherton and (no sniggering at the front) Paul Collingwood. Even Chris Tavare makes the grade. As Gideon Haigh, the English-born, Australian-bred cricket writer who surely ranks among Tavare's most ardent fans, once put it: 'He did not so much score runs as smuggle them out by stealth.' Australians find it mystifying that someone like Tavare should inspire such affection. But for the English his strokelessness was taken as an insane devotion to the cause. Heck, at least he wasn't doing anything too over the top like attempting to hit a boundary. Perhaps we're back to Gill: 'The English teeter on the edge of not being able to take anything seriously.' And that includes choosing their cricketing heroes.

This instinctive siding with the artisans over the artists – it was a crime for Gower to fiddle outside off-stump, but a mere lapse when Tavare chose to do so – expresses itself in other ways. When the nation was debating whether to pick Kevin Pietersen for the 2005 Ashes in place of Graham Thorpe (another nuggety battler), there was a lot of typically English concern about Pietersen's bottom-handed tendencies. Never mind the fact that he had just averaged over 150 in a losing cause during a one-day series in his native – and extremely hostile – South Africa. No, what the self-appointed aficionados of technique wanted to know was: would he breach a little-read page of the MCC's coaching manual and play across the line against Glenn McGrath? He did, and it cost him his wicket. But not before he had made 158 on the last day of the series to wrestle back the Ashes for the first time in sixteen years. So they had a go at his earring and his haircut instead.

Yes, the English love a cricketer who goes in for self-deprecation. At the ICC World Twenty20 in South Africa in 2007, incoming batsmen introduced themselves to the camera via a prerecorded message. Asked to name his favourite shot, Collingwood twinkled: 'The nurdle on the leg-side.' But get all cocky and start scoring Ashes-winning hundreds and, frankly, you deserve everything that comes to you. That 5–0 humiliation eighteen months later felt far more like it.

India

Three press-box buddies and I once flagged down a small van that was masquerading as a taxi in the streets of Delhi. We were all in a rush to get back to our hotel and write up our reports of a comedy England defeat, but the taxi got stuck at what I still believe to be the slowest set of traffic lights in the known universe. As we sat there for fifteen minutes, breathing in the fumes and wilting like pathetic Englishmen in the late-March heat, the engine started to make a funny noise. 'No problem,' said our driver, a huge Sikh who didn't look as if people generally disagreed with him. But there *was* a problem and it didn't sound good. As soon as we had passed the lights from hell our driver pulled over at the first available fountain. He scurried off to find a bucket – like fountains, these are surprisingly ready to hand in the streets of Delhi – which he filled with water and brought back to his wheezing vehicle. Now, the engine was located under the passenger seat in the front, so while one of us – the one who didn't fancy having his backside toasted – made room, the other three wrenched back the seat as the big man tipped the contents of the bucket over the steaming engine, then stood back to admire his handiwork. It proved rudimentary but effective, rather like an Ian Blackwell innings at Taunton. 'Are you sure this car isn't going to blow up?' one of us asked. And then he did it. That funny little head wobble that means either yes or no or haven't the foggiest, and occasionally all three. No one said a word. We were in our driver's hairy hands. But I was more interested in his head. Because if one gesture could sum up Indian cricket, this was it.

India has never been short of cricketing talent. Take a stroll across Shivaji Park in Mumbai, the dusty maidan where the young Sachin Tendulkar learned how to reduce bowlers to tears by working balls from outside off-stump through midwicket, and you can spot more natural ability than at the average county second XI net session. But for many years, until Sourav Ganguly grabbed the Indian game by the scruff of the neck and turned the ambivalent head wobble into a vigorous nod, that talent was almost apologetic. Fatalism ruled. If a half-volley was driven to third slip, then it was simply meant to be. Further analysis was futile. In *Cricket Wallah*, Scyld Berry's superb account of England's trip to India in 1981–82, the full force of the fatalistic head wobble was to be found in the court-jester batting of Kris Srikkanth. Every time he played a shot of which his more methodical batting partner, Sunil Gavaskar, disapproved, 'Gavaskar would walk down the pitch to speak to him, not criticising his boldness but simply telling him to keep his concentration going.' Berry goes on to describe how Srikkanth would 'silently wobble-shake his head from side to side', and then – bravely – he offers an interpretation. 'Yes, captain, what you say is indeed understood and I appreciate your telling me this. However, although we may

44

agree about the end, we may differ as to the means. For the moment what more can I say than that I will try to heed your advice?' Simon Hughes argues in *Yakking Around the World* that the only way of deciphering the wobble 'is by looking at the raised/lowered eyebrows'. Quite possibly. But if Gavaskar possessed the kind of methodical temperament more readily associated with the white cricket nations, then Srikkanth was the classic Indian, abnegating responsibility and surrendering himself to kismet.

Anyone who has spent more than five minutes on an Indian road will know that such a view is not limited to the cricket field. (The key to emerging from a rickshaw ride with your bladder still intact and your legs feeling more supportive than spaghetti is to pretend the whole thing is a computer game. You're unlikely to get hit, because the driver tends to value his own life too, so you may as well enjoy the ride.) But Ganguly decided enough was enough. Taking over the captaincy in 2000, he immediately set about making a mockery of the claim by Lord Harris, a pompous former Governor of Bombay, that Indians would never make decent cricketers because they lacked 'Anglo-Saxon phlegm'. Ganguly convinced his own side that they did not need to grow a moustache the size of a small walrus to sledge opponents. He burrowed under skin so successfully that the otherwise unflappable Steve Waugh called him a 'prick' and the English journalist Michael Henderson – opera lover and general bon viveur – repeatedly referred to him in print as Lord Snooty. The vehemence stemmed in part from the surprise: Indian cricketers were supposed to play beautifully for 100, then chop an off-break enigmatically to slip. They were not supposed to turn up late for the toss and celebrate a wicket with a pump of the fist. These days, the Indians are even producing snarling young fast bowlers, which for batsmen must feel like being slapped in the chops by the local vicar. One of them, Sreesanth, went even further during a Test match in Johannesburg in 2006. He had been getting some dreadful stick from the South African fast bowler Andre Nel, a madman off the field and less sane on it, where he blames his behaviour on a mountain-dwelling, oxygen-starved alter ego called Gunther. Sreesanth's response to his ear-bending was to drive Nel/Gunther back over his head for six, at which point he did something very strange. He rotated his hips like a professional belly dancer and waved his bat round his head like a lasso, prancing down the pitch in the direction of the chastened Nel. Better than the head wobble, anyway. And by the time India arrived for their tour of Australia in 2007–08, they were giving as good as they got.

One thing hasn't changed, though. No other group, with the possible exception of Trekkies and Captain Spock, venerates the cult of the individual as highly as the Indians. Ganguly went some way towards superimposing a team ethic, but personal milestones tend to delight Indian fans almost as much as team success. Just look at Sachin Tendulkar. At the time of writing Sachin had hit a world-record thirty-nine Test hundreds, but only thirteen of them had come in an Indian win. Yet if you make this point as I have just done – soberly and empirically – you are likely to receive emails from all over the Indian subcontinent gently advising you to 'go fuck yourself, you great bustard [*sic*]'. Now, I am not for one moment suggesting these people represent India. They do not. They are the definitive small but vociferous minority. But how small and how vociferous! When I was working for *Wisden*, our website compiled a list of the 100 greatest Test innings ever played. The list was based on a complicated system designed by – you guessed it – an Indian, who factored in everything from the quality of the opposition to the nature of the pitch, via the match situation and which side of bed the batsman had emerged from that morning. Not a single one of Tendulkar's innings made it. The scale of the Indian outrage was genuinely disconcerting, and I'm not sure my inbox ever recovered from the shock.

New Zealand

To understand what makes the average New Zealand cricketer's hackles rise, just titter patronisingly at the kiwi. While the English have the lion, the Australians the kangaroo and the South Africans the springbok, the New Zealanders have a half-blind bird that cannot fly and snuffles about in the undergrowth in search of prey that deserves to take a long, hard look at itself should it ever be caught by this limping quarter-wit of a creature. Perhaps sensing the inherent absurdity of the situation, the New Zealanders decided to rename their cricket team the Black Caps, a cunning variant on their greatest national export, the All Blacks, and one which has been applied to the nation's footballers (the All Whites), basketball team (the Tall Blacks) and badminton players (the – what else? – Black Cocks). No matter that the new name was straight out of the Genghis Khan school of sophistication: the name Black Caps was supposed to lend an air of menace. Yet this was as futile as trying to get Americans interested in soccer. The truth is – and this is going to hurt me more than it hurts the Kiwis – that it has always been difficult to take New Zealand seriously as a cricket nation.

Part of this stems from the fact that the All Blacks nick all the country's best sportsmen, then teach them the words to a scary song called the haka which makes every other sporting occasion in New Zealand seem like a Women's Institute AGM. Here's Brian O'Driscoll, who captained the British and Irish Lions rugby team to New Zealand in 2005: 'Having been here six weeks, I would say that their obsession with rugby borders on the unhealthy. Being passionate about something is fine, but rugby dominates to the exclusion of everything else. This results in tunnel vision. There has to be life outside rugby, especially in such a gorgeous country with everything going for it.' It goes without saying that O'Driscoll ended up both in hospital and on the losing side. But the main issue here is that – rugby aside – New Zealand's society is riddled with an all-pervading sense of unworthiness which may or may not have something to do with constant references to the place as 'a small island nation off the east coast of Tasmania'.

If you type 'New Zealand inferiority complex' into Google, you will find – assuming your PC does not crash in the process – 52,800 results, a figure which Australian sociologists believe will have reached the 100,000 mark by the time you read this. One report, based on the number of times the word 'lonely' was entered into internet search engines, identified Auckland as the third most isolated city on the planet (after, bizarrely, Dublin and Melbourne). And on his trip to Wellington, one of the least ostentatious capital cities in the western world, Michael Palin lapped up the sun and the cleanliness before noting: 'Something is missing and the New Zealanders know it. They want more than all this. In the bedrooms of the comfortable villas of Kelburn, teenagers are making plans to get out – to Africa, America and Europe. Young New Zealanders want excitement.'

New Zealand cricketers want more than that. They long to be respected, but this is not always easy. If a team could choose a number with which to be associated, they would probably go for a nice, round, fat 100. New Zealand's less glamorous fate is to be linked to the number 26. This is the total – still the lowest in Test history – they were bowled out for by England at Auckland in 1955. It is the number of years they needed to win their first Test (Bangladesh needed only four and a bit years to win theirs). And it is also thought to be the average age at which a New Zealand cricketer begins to wonder whether he should jack it all in and instead become Manawatu rugby club's fifteenth-choice scrum-half, a position which is far more likely to bring him fame and fortune than opening the batting for the Black Caps.

New Zealand's simmering resentment over its lack of status can go one of two ways. Either their players fall into line with what the rest of the world thinks and retreat into mild-mannered self-deprecation, a process which includes laughing along at predictable gags about their clipped – 'clupped' – vowels. Or they become extraordinarily chippy ('chuppy'; I'll stop now). The *Daily Telegraph* cricket writer Martin Johnson used to take great delight in his portrayals of New Zzzzzealand and their unique brand of slow-medium dibbly-dobblers. His view, hammed up with typical wit for the benefit of his readers, was that nothing encapsulated the Kiwis' lack of charisma more than the sight of Gavin Larsen floating down 70 mph seamers designed to take a batsman's wicket by sending him to sleep. But the joke was not appreciated by Larsen. When Johnson, who had been watching New Zealand play Zimbabwe in the 1999 World Cup, wrote that 'the idea of Larsen and Harris bowling to Goodwin and Campbell isn't calculated to cause a stampede at the turnstiles – not to get in, anyway,' Larsen was not amused. In his autobiography, he called Johnson's article 'the most derogatory and patronising piece I've seen written on the New Zealand cricket team'. Which presumably meant he hadn't read the rest of Johnson's work.

Even Stephen Fleming, a man who did more than anyone to add a layer of toughness to New Zealand's exterior, occasionally cracked under the strain. After his side won in England in 1999, he was flabbergasted by the lack of credit they received from the press. 'It was bloody annoying at times, the reporting,' he would write several years later. 'It didn't matter what we did, the English media couldn't see anything good in us. It was about how badly they'd played and not much else, and that ticked us off – almost to a man.' (I love the 'almost to a man' – a classic example of Kiwi aggression falling flat.) Worse was to follow when Fleming took over the captaincy of Nottinghamshire in 2005. The fact that he would spend the summer leading the county to their first championship title since 1987 was not enough to please most journalists. No, all they wanted to know was who he thought would win the Ashes. For a New Zealander, it was the ultimate insult: a reminder of their position on the periphery, and of two of their most recent results (0–3 in England and 0–2 at home to Australia). It was a bit like asking the leader of the

Liberal Democrats which of Labour or the Conservatives was going to win the next election.

I feel sorry for the Kiwis, I mean the Black Caps. I have spent two very happy tours there, and find their people incredibly friendly, their air clean, their food delicious, their wine crisp and their traffic jams non-existent. They just never seem to get the credit they deserve. Richard Hadlee was one of the most incisively brilliant bowlers in the history of the game, but is he ever spoken of in the same awed breath as Dennis Lillee or Michael Holding? Even the compliments are double-edged. Graham Gooch, who fell to Hadlee twice as often as he did to any of his team-mates, reckoned that batting against New Zealand was a case of 'The World XI at one end and Ilford Seconds at the other'. Then there was Mark Greatbatch, who invented pinch-hitting at the 1992 World Cup watched helplessly as history attributed the first use of the tactic to the Sri Lankan openers Sanath Jayasuriya and Romesh Kaluwitharana in 1996. And only in New Zealand could a team's greatest-ever innings have been played in a losing cause. I was at Christchurch that day when Nathan Astle took England for 222 off 168 balls, with 28 fours and 11 sixes. His second century came off 39 deliveries, but the best statistic was the maiden in Andy Caddick's spell of 3-1-45-1. England won by 98 runs and a nation didn't know whether to laugh or cry. Then they all shrugged their shoulders and went home to see if there was any rugby on the telly. Which there almost certainly was.

Pakistan

If I had been paid a pound every time I read that the Pakistanis would be world champions if only they could harness their natural talent, I would be far away on a desert island chuckling at the prospect of ever needing to write a book to earn a living. Because Pakistan, you see, would be world champions if only they could harness their natural talent. Like Kevin Pietersen's fashion blunders and Shane Warne's double chin, it is one of cricket's facts of life. Over the years, the Pakistanis have redefined bathos not merely by veering from the sublime to the ridiculous but by squeezing a whole host of other abstract nouns into the process too. To call them the Keystone Cops of the international circuit would be to confer a frankly flattering sense of organisation on a team that has been accused of match-fixing, ball-tampering and drug-taking, sometimes, it feels, in the same day. To label them 'mercurial', as many do, is to suggest quite misleadingly that their essence can be reduced to one element alone. Perhaps Duncan Fletcher's favourite word fits best: multi-dimensional. They are never dull, and if they were, you would suspect it was because they simply didn't feel like being colourful.

However capable they are of being bowled out for 59 and 53 by Australia only two Tests after compiling 643 against New Zealand, I grew up fearing the Pakistan team far more than India. They didn't do the head wobble for starters, which for a young westerner meant they were probably quite hard. They also tended to win in England, which India, back then in any case, did not. And they produced frightening fast bowlers capable of reverse-swinging the old ball at 90 mph onto the tip of your big toe and the base of the stumps at the same time.

In *Pundits from Pakistan*, the Indian writer Rahul Bhattacharya asks the former Pakistan fast bowler Aqib Javed why it is that India has always lagged behind their great rivals in the pace stakes. Part of the reason, replies Aqib, is diet: Pakistanis, as Muslims, eat beef; Indians, four-fifths of them Hindus, do not. 'The aggression,' says Aqib, 'you get that from the beef.' He goes on: 'Your Srinath, he was 90 miles [*sic*], but he never created terror. His body language was so soft. My speed was less than his. But the pressure I could exert, because of my body language, was much more.'

Whatever the supernatural powers of beef and – as Aqib also suggests – buffalo meat, Pakistan's long tradition of fast bowlers, from Fazal Mahmood in the 1950s via Imran Khan and Sarfraz Nawaz in the 1970s and '80s, through to Wasim Akram, Waqar Younis and Shoaib Akhtar, has always given them the capacity to turn a game that seems to be heading nowhere.

Then there is the question of reverse swing, fast bowling's most treasured sleight of hand, which is achieved by different means depending on who is doing it – or, perhaps more to the point, who is writing about it. When Pakistan won in England in 1992, the cry of 'cheat', perhaps preceded by an insulting epithet, was never far away, particularly in the British tabloids. But when England employed reverse swing to beat Australia in 2005, they were praised for their ingenuity. A claim by an Australian that the English had been sucking on sweets to provide a sugary coat of saliva to apply to the ball – God forbid – was dismissed, inappropriately, as sour grapes. Still, most people accepted that reverse swing was a Pakistani gift to the game, honed in the 1970s, so the story went, by Sarfraz and handed down the generations like a meaningless trinket in a Dan Brown novel. The secrecy was sacrosanct and did little to distract from accusations of skulduggery. Not so long ago, I was talking to Geoff Arnold, the Surrey bowling coach who played thirty-four Tests for England. 'Reverse swing is nothing new,' he said casually. 'Mushtaq Mohammad said he first encountered it when I was bowling on the 1972–73 tour of Pakistan.' Come again? Was Arnold, a reliably English type of seam bowler, claiming to have invented reverse swing? Damn right he was! 'I tried to shine one side with a lot of sweat and kept the other side dry. I suddenly discovered it was going the other way from what I thought. It really happened on the off-chance.' So there you had it. If what Arnold was saying was correct, it was all an Englishman's fault anyway, which feels like precisely the kind of surprise Pakistani cricket has always dealt in.

Of all the Pakistanis who fascinated me when I was a kid, Javed Miandad usually won hands down. Journalistic convention had it that Miandad, a magnificent batsman, should be referred to as a 'streetfighter', which – as with so many tags applied by the western media to subcontinental cricketers – managed to be a compliment and sound mildly patronising at the same time. Yet it had the ring of truth: Javed specialised in squeezing the most out of a situation through the kind of sheer nerve that would not have come naturally to an Indian. Take the second Test against Australia at Faisalabad in March 1980. Pakistan had won the first and were so keen to hold on to their advantage that when light drizzle began to fall after Greg Chappell had won the toss, Javed refused to bring his team out to play. For the entire day. Chappell was so incensed that he set about compiling a double century in a total of 617 before bowling all eleven of his players as the match petered out into a farcical draw, exactly as Javed wanted. He was also, the story goes, instrumental in exploiting the Gatting-Shakoor Rana affair eight years later, to ensure a day was lost at Faisalabad – another occasion on which Pakistan held a series lead. It was gamesmanship of the highest class. But he could be straightforward too. Fortunate to survive a shout for lbw at a crucial stage of the 1992 World Cup final, he approached the bowler, Derek Pringle after the match. He tapped his ankle and said with a wink: 'Allah was with me today.'

I loved Javed. He was argumentative, feisty, brilliant enough to hit the last ball of a one-day international against India in Sharjah for six when four would have done, and more inventive than any English cricketer could ever dream of being. The only surprise when chaos descended that day at The Oval in 2006 after Darrell Hair had penalised the Pakistanis for alleged ball-tampering was that Javed wasn't in the middle of it all, pulling the strings. Although perhaps, in a strange kind of way, he was.

South Africa

First, an admission. My entire view of South African cricketers will be forever blighted by Gary Kirsten's double century at Old Trafford in 1998. Now, before giant men called Johannes and Pieter start spluttering at me in something sounding like Dutch, I should point out that Kirsten himself described his innings of 210, chiselled out

in 10 hours and 50 minutes from 525 balls, as the worst of
his life. Don't for one moment imagine this was false
modesty. Kirsten had batted for roughly the time it takes to
fly from Heathrow to his home city of Cape Town, but for
a penniless graduate earning some post-university pocket
money in the local Co-op freezer-warehouse there were no
on-flight miniature vodkas or sachets of pretzels to ease the
pain. This was South African dourness at its most
expressive, or possibly its least. And because England
eventually saved that game with one wicket in hand, and
went on to win at Trent Bridge and Headingley, there is a
strong case for arguing that Kirsten's sloth cost South
Africa the series. For a 23-year-old like me who had never
rejoiced in a major England series win it was all too
delicious for words.

South Africa have had their share of attacking
cricketers, but – even accepting the arrival on the scene of
Dale Steyn – how many of those have come since 1991,
when they were readmitted into the international fold?
Herschelle Gibbs, granted. And Jonty Rhodes, although for
all the hyperactivity he made only three Test hundreds.
Certainly Allan Donald, who was the fastest white bowler
alive at his peak. But the image of the left-handed Kirsten
propping forward in his dark-green helmet to smother
another half-volley and then gathering his strength for the
next maiden has proved a little too definitive for South
Africa's good. From Kepler Wessels via Hansie Cronje to
Graeme Smith, conservatism has run through their
approach like a set of grumpy babushka dolls. It's a
macabre thought that the most enterprising declaration
ever undertaken by a South African captain came at
Centurion in January 2000, when Cronje's motivation to

make a game of it came from a fistful of rand and a leather
jacket.

I have tried – goodness knows I have tried! – to give
the South Africans the benefit of the doubt, and I generally
cheer them on against Australia, if only on a lesser-of-two-
evils basis. But their fate was sealed in my mind by Jacques
Kallis's performance in the Sydney Test of January 2006.
South Africa were one down with one to play and needed
quick runs on the fifth morning to set Australia a target. So
what did Kallis do? Yep, he batted for three hours to make
an unbeaten 50 while his team-mates and extras chipped in
with 138 at the other end. Worse, his captain Smith was
prepared to delay his declaration until Kallis had reached
this piddling milestone, as if he was waiting for him to
conquer Everest or split the atom rather than boost his
Test average by 0.38. Australia knocked off the runs for the
loss of two wickets and Kallis left the pavilion by the back
door. Or at least he should have done.

This South African tentativeness probably stems from
fear of defeat, which paradoxically stems from a desire to
win and then overwhelms it. For South Africans are as
competitive as they come. Jasper Carrott once invented a
character called Wiggy, who would dress his three-year-old
son in cricket gear, bowl at him from about 10 yards in the
back garden, and sink to his knees in jubilation as the
middle stump cartwheeled into the begonias. The South
Africans frequently resemble a team of Wiggies. In 2007,
Herschelle Gibbs bullied six sixes in an over off Daan van
Bunge, a leg-spinner from the Netherlands. But that was
small fry compared with 2004, when New Zealand's Mark
Richardson invited the least mobile member of the South
African squad to take part in a 100-metre sprint. The joke

was that Richardson was the least mobile biped in the southern hemisphere, but South Africa – possibly piqued by failing to win the Test series – sent forth the whippet-like Neil McKenzie, who duly zigzagged his way to victory. It was like cheating at Monopoly against your grandma.

A lot of South Africa's seriousness was instilled by Hansie Cronje. It always astonished me that Cronje would be held up as a paragon, even in the days before his involvement with the bookies made cricket fans look at life a little more suspiciously. If anyone embodied South Africa's win-at-all-costs attitude, their Protestant work ethic, their grim seriousness (and other assorted clichés), it was the man with the broodingly bushy eyebrows and the aura of invincibility. On a tour of Australia in 1997–98, Cronje twice showed the darker side of his character. First he was filmed standing on the ball with his spikes, as blatant an example of tampering as you can get without hacking the ball to shreds with a machete while grinning at the camera. Then he slammed a stump through the door of the umpires' dressing room after they had failed to give out Mark Waugh hit-wicket during the third Test at Adelaide. Waugh went on to score a match-saving, series-winning century. At the time of writing, South Africa are still awaiting their first series win over Australia since they beat them 4–0 in 1969–70. It rankles.

But it doesn't rankle half as much as their exits from the 1999 and 2003 World Cups. On both occasions they fell one run short of victory in comical circumstances. Lance Klusener and Allan Donald were more like Laurel and Hardy than Sutcliffe and Hobbs as they made a complete hash of trying to score the winning run in the 1999 semi-final against Australia at Edgbaston. Four years later, the team misread their Duckworth/Lewis charts and were knocked out of the group stages by Sri Lanka at Durban. It's strange to relate, but this haplessness is another strange feature of the South African cricketing psyche. The Aussies have delighted in calling them chokers because they know it gets under South African skin. The South Africans know the accusation contains a grain of truth, which bugs them all the more.

Sri Lanka

Imagine spending most of your childhood having sand kicked in your face. One day you decide you can't take it any more. You disappear from the beach circuit, spend months in the gym and return to break the legs of your tormentors with your bare hands. Give or take a snapped limb or two, that is the tale of the emergence of the Sri Lankan cricket team, and it has left them with an identity crisis that has never quite been adequately resolved. Are they the happy-go-lucky islanders whose old Arabic name of Serendip bespeaks a tendency to rely on fortunate discoveries, like Muttiah Muralitharan's wrist or Arjuna Ranatunga's abnormally thick skin? Or are they a bunch of ruthless young thrusters determined never to return to the days of seaside subservience? Sociologists are yet to reach a conclusion.

At times the Sri Lankans have suffered from the same credibility problem as the New Zealanders. In neither case has it helped to be on the doorstep of the world's two cricketing superpowers, even though Sri Lanka has never been as obsessed with India as New Zealand is with Australia. But the Sri Lankans have gone about asserting themselves without tacit need for approval. And they have done this mainly because of the two men name-checked in the previous paragraph. If Muralitharan has been the star turn, taking roughly two-fifths of all Sri Lanka's wickets since he first let the world in on his rubbery wrist and goggle eyes in 1992, then Ranatunga was his big, brassy agent, a barrel-chested general of a man whose sole aim in life, it seemed, was to kick the sand back with interest. Others, such as Aravinda de Silva, Sanath Jayasuriya and Chaminda Vaas, have sparkled quite beautifully, but none has exerted the pulling power of Murali or the charisma of Ranatunga. And none has been no-balled for throwing by self-congratulatory Australian umpires or called a 'fat [expletive deleted]' by an Australian wicketkeeper.

Until 1972, Sri Lanka was referred to by the outside world as Ceylon, because that's what the British called it. In cricketing terms it was a stopping-off point for England and Australia teams seeking a break as they sailed halfway round the world to play for the Ashes. Attitudes towards the Sinhalese, as they were known before independence, were warm but – from a 21st-century perspective – a touch un-PC. Here's Jack Fingleton, who opened for Australia in the 1930s, describing a crowd scene in Colombo in his book *Brightly Fades the Don*, an account of the 1948 Ashes series. 'You see thousands of dark, smiling faces against a background of gleaming teeth and the startling white of their dress. The enthusiasm of the Colombo crowd is infectious. They applaud vigorously, chit-chat about every little incident and laugh uproariously at anything which tickles their fancy – and plenty does.' The subtext is not hard to discern: simple folk enjoying simple pleasures. And until Sri Lanka started winning Test matches on a reasonably regular basis in the 1990s, the accusation of naivety stuck like Marvan Atapattu in one of his less skittish moods.

But Ranatunga moved Sri Lanka on from the idea that their role was to be a bunch of amiable losers. Ranatunga would have made a perfect Toad of Toad Hall in a Sri Lankan production of *The Wind in the Willows*. He was never happier than when strutting around the field barking orders, mainly to his own team, but occasionally to the umpires. When Ross Emerson no-balled Murali for throwing during a one-day game against England at Adelaide, Ranatunga led his players off the pitch. When they returned, he instructed Emerson to stand closer to the stumps, a tactic designed to prevent him from getting a good look at Murali's action. Later in the same game, Roshan Mahanama barged Darren Gough out of the way as Gough tried to gather the ball for a quick run-out, prompting Gough to feign a headbutt. England's captain Alec Stewart was so irritated by the whole thing that he made a mess of his attempted sledge to Ranatunga. 'Your behaviour today has been appalling for a county country captain,' he said, to general bemusement. Stewart later wrote that Ranatunga was 'the only cricketer who's ever wound me up on the field with his antics'.

The point was that Sri Lanka had moved on from the days when it was acceptable to talk of their dark, smiling faces and gleaming teeth. They could still be charming, of course. After all, what other Test team could boast an opening bowler who sang love songs to his wife with as much élan as Vaas? And was Kumar Sangakkara the only wicketkeeper in the world who could lose himself in the works of Oscar Wilde? But Ranatunga had instilled a refusal to be cowed: his verbal battles with Shane Warne, usually involving accusations of who had swallowed how much of what, were the stuff of legend. And the legend lived on long after his retirement in 2000. Mike Atherton described England's tour of Sri Lanka later that year as the most acrimonious he had ever played in. Helmets were flung, fingers pointed, umpires bullied, insults exchanged, and that was just at the toss. There were even claims during a warm-up match at Matara that Ruchira Perera had directed racist abuse at Craig White, although the more sober analysis was that Perera had probably said something involving White's surname.

Still, let's give credit where it's due, as Ranatunga almost certainly never said. Before Sri Lanka won their third Test, against New Zealand in 1992–93, their overall record was P41 W2 L20 D19. Since then, up to and including their tour of the Caribbean in early 2008, they have won 49 and lost 46 of their 135 Tests. They have also lifted a World Cup, won a Test series against Australia and sparked countless jokes, mainly from Englishmen, about the unpronounceability of their surnames.

Tim Rice, the former president of the MCC, tells a story about the time he was roped in to commentate for *Test Match Special* in a game involving the Sri Lankans. Since Rice had once confused Gladstone Small with Graham Gooch live on air, the portents were not good, and he spent his entire stint at the microphone praying for the ball to be hit to the Sri Lankan seamer Vinothen John. 'That would have been easily fielded had the ball gone to John,' he would say as Don Anurasiri or Rumesh Ratnayake did the honours. 'Time for Duleep Mendis to give John a bowl,' he would declaim as his co-commentator gently pointed out that John had completed his spell some time ago. Nowadays, you poke fun at your peril.

West Indies

No team, not even England, has undergone a more severe transformation in the past fifteen years than West Indies. It has been Trinny and Susannah in reverse, stripping an ageing Hell's Angel of his shiny leather jacket and sending him out in public wearing sackcloth and ashes. And it has provoked endless shakes of the head by lovers of the game, who all agree, without knowing exactly why, that world cricket 'needs a strong West Indies'. For many years it was a sentiment that made little sense to me. I have vague and disquieting memories of their 4–0 win in England in 1988, when the home selectors warmed up for the shameful 29-man Ashes summer of '89 by choosing four different captains. And I was outraged when England were denied an incredible 2–0 lead in Trinidad in 1989–90 by some West Indian time-wasting which seemed to involve Curtly Ambrose continually doing up his shoelaces (very fiddly they were too). But by 2000, Andy Caddick was taking four wickets in an over at Headingley. By 2004, Steve Harmison was claiming 7 for 12 in Jamaica. Later that year England were whitewashing them 4–0. The worm had not merely turned. It had performed a triple salchow. Yes, one thing is for sure: world cricket needs a strong West Indies, even if it is with the help of a Texan billionaire.

It is generally agreed that West Indies' global reign of terror ended in 1995, when Mark Taylor's team won 2–1 in the Caribbean. But for me reality did not sink in until England visited in 1998. True, West Indies won the series

3–1. Yet for the last two Tests they selected Philo Wallace and Clayton Lambert, a pair of openers whose idea of taking the shine off the new ball revolved around belting it into the nearby streets. In his 1966 essay, 'Kanhai: A Study in Confidence', the Trinidadian historian and cricket lover C.L.R. James wrestled with the essence of his favourite team. 'The West Indies in my view embody more sharply than elsewhere Nietzsche's conflict between the ebullience of Dionysus and the discipline of Apollo,' he declared, as numerous workaday hacks prepared to sue for plagiarism. Wallace and Lambert must have stopped reading after the mention of Dionysus: they tried to smash everything, and briefly succeeded. Angus Fraser became so fed up with being dumped back over his head in comedy fashion that he christened the pair 'Wallace and Gromit'. Neither had an extended career: Wallace was dropped soon afterwards (he scored 68 runs in eight innings on a tour of South Africa), while Lambert was politely shown the door after making 43 in four. Gordon Greenidge and Desmond Haynes they assuredly were not. The golden age was over.

The decline and fall was evident in the bowlers too. It used to be the case that Clive Lloyd or Viv Richards merely had to work out a rota for their four world-class quicks. This usually took about five seconds, after which the likes of Andy Roberts, Michael Holding, Joel Garner, Colin Croft, Malcolm Marshall, Ian Bishop, Courtney Walsh or Curtly Ambrose would bowl eleven overs an hour of chin music designed, as Haynes once put it, to take the batsman 'up to the twelfth floor'. Yes, batting against West Indies could be a lonely business. 'One of the disconcerting things about facing the Windies' ultra-quicks on their own lightning-fast tracks,' wrote Graham Gooch, 'is that no fielder is in front of the bat, so it's as if you're the only one in the spotlight – you are too, for that matter – because all that's in vision is the umpire, the non-striker and the bowler steaming in. You know the ring of five slips, two gullies and two leg-slips or whatever is behind you in a cordon, but you never actually look at them. You just hear them.' It's little wonder that of the nineteen Tests spread across four series between West Indies and England in the 1980s, West Indies won sixteen and, to their disgust, drew three.

When West Indies arrived in England in 2000, things had changed. Ambrose and Walsh remained, but their support came from the likes of Reon King, Nixon McLean and Franklyn Rose. In a five-Test series won 3–1 by England, Walsh and Ambrose bowled more than 400 overs between them for a return of 51 wickets; the other three managed 19 wickets in 200 overs. Things got so bad that Ambrose, a man who rarely bothered to open his mouth unless he was appealing for lbw, denounced his team-mates in a Channel 4 interview conducted by his former team-mate Ian Bishop. My abiding memory from that series is of Rose, having delivered some twelfth-man drinks to a team-mate, disrupting play by absent-mindedly walking in front of the sightscreen behind the bowler's arm like a confused pensioner. It was a moment that seemed to sum up West Indies' new-found carelessness, and some believe the series turned when Rose tried and failed to bounce out Dominic Cork during England's two-wicket win in the second Test at Lord's. Since then, England have beaten West Indies 3–0, 4–0 and 3–0. It was hard to find any of the England players agreeing that world cricket needed a strong West Indies.

Much has been made of the reasons behind their

decline: the increasing gravitation towards all things American, although Sir Allen Stanford might have something to say about that; the lack of forward planning in the days when the team swept all before them; a questionable work ethic that some are apt to romanticise by placing it alongside coconut trees and rum punches as an integral part of the Caribbean character; social problems that make things such as cricket seem trivial. The truth, though, is probably that the West Indian dominance of international cricket between the 1980s and early 1990s was one of sport's great freaks: rarely have so many talents emerged at one time from such a small space. By 2005 expectations had changed so radically that I – a medium-pace trundler of little guile – was daring to give tips to Ian Bishop, one of the greatest fast bowlers in the history of the game. Bishop was struggling to get rid of a stubborn left-handed opener during a match in Kent for the Cricket Writers' Club. 'Aim for the stumps!' I suggested from mid-off, as one delivery after another sailed through at chest height to the wicket-keeper. 'I'm trying, man, I'm trying,' said Bishop, possessor of 161 Test wickets at an average of 24. Moments later he pitched one up and scattered the timber. Yes, when my wrists give way, my eyes fail and the clichés dry up, I will go into coaching.

Zimbabwe

They might be pretty useless right now, but there was a time, in the mid-1990s, when the English were in no position to mock. If one game could have summed up the Ealing-comedy hopelessness of the England team in that period it was the 131-run defeat to Zimbabwe in the third one-day international at Harare in January 1997. It was bad enough that England were already 2–0 down in the three-match series to a side that had won seven games in the previous thirteen years. What made it all the more harrowing was that defeat was hastened by a hat-trick from Eddo Brandes, a typically burly Zimbabwean who farmed chickens in his spare time, which – given Zimbabwe's lack of fixtures – was most of it. England's miserable state of mind at the time was reflected by the fact that when Brandes took his third wicket (Nasser Hussain caught behind), the batsman did not even realise he had helped complete a hat-trick. Mike Atherton later wrote of Brandes: 'When he wasn't feeding his chooks, he was a fine outswing bowler.' But that was of no account to the British media, who went understandably big on the poultry angle.

In many ways Brandes was the archetypal Zimbabwean in the days before corruption and racism tore apart the team and eventually deprived them of Test status. He was competitive, uncompromising, loved getting one over the English and could banter with the best of them. His supposed retort to Glenn McGrath about biscuits has done the email rounds too many times to bear repetition here, but it is already part of sledging's hall of fame. Brandes was helped by playing in a side that formed part of Zimbabwe's golden era. Sure, they had beaten Australia in the 1983 World Cup, mainly thanks to a glittering all-round per-formance from the future England coach, Duncan Fletcher. But even that couldn't compare with the heady days of Dave Houghton, Alistair Campbell, Henry Olonga, Heath Streak and an assortment of brothers called Flower, Strang, Whittall and Rennie.

Most of these characters were playing in the infamous

'flippin' murdered 'em' match against England at Bulawayo in December 1996, when for the first time a Test finished as a tie with the scores level. The quote comes from the England coach David Lloyd, a delightful man who has since carved out a successful career as the funniest commentator in cricket broadcasting, but who at the time was incensed by Zimbabwe's tactics of bowling sufficiently wide of the stumps to prevent England's batsmen reaching the ball but not so wide that the umpires penalised them. Lloyd did not merely wear his heart on his sleeve: he tattooed it to his forehead. Later that winter, after England had wasted the new ball on the opening morning of a Test at Auckland, Lloyd was so furious that he sat outside the dressing room for the entire lunch break. Now, with defeats to Mashonaland and in the first one-day international already under England's belt, his frustrations spilled over and out popped a line that is to Lloyd what 'Kiss me, Hardy' was to Nelson.

The tour ranks among England's unhappiest. They were accused of adopting what is usually called a 'siege mentality' (what does this mean? Did they hoard bread and water?), although Lloyd later defended this by saying that 'the truth in my view is that Harare is the pits'. Things got so bad that when the team arrived in New Zealand for the second leg of the winter, Atherton was faced with ITN's news reporter, Michael Nicholson, who promptly questioned his suitability for the job. Atherton noted that Nicholson was on stand-by to fly to Russia, where Boris Yeltsin was teetering on the brink. 'I fervently wished Boris would take a turn for the worse,' he would later write.

If much of the last paragraph feels a touch Anglo-centric for a section that is supposed to be about

68

Zimbabwe, then I hope Zimbabwean readers will take this as a compliment. Because until England started pummelling their weakened side on a regular basis from around 1999 onwards, the Zimbabweans were something of a bête noire. They were one of only two sides to beat England in the nine-team round robin of the 1992 World Cup, and helped knock them out of the 1994–95 Benson & Hedges World Series, a tournament whose name was belied by the fact that the final ended up being contested by Australia and Australia A. By the time Zimbabwe had whitewashed England in the one-dayers on the flippin'-murdered-'em tour two years later, they had won five of their six ODIs against the mother country. Their motivation was fairly straightforward: England had blocked their ascent to Test level and messages to that effect were posted on Zimbabwe's dressing-room walls. Even when their team was disintegrating amid a mess of politically motivated selections and mass defections by their white players, Zimbabwe still seemed to act as England's nemesis: the refusal of Nasser Hussain's side to fulfil their World Cup fixture against them in Harare in 2003 in effect cost them their place in the competition.

By now, the golden age was long gone, even if the southern African competitive spirit remained. 'We hate to lose, and we don't like drawing,' explained their left-arm spinner Ray Price in 2003. 'You should see our guys play tiddlywinks.' At the time of writing, tiddlywinks is being played more often than the Zimbabweans would wish. They have not played a Test since September 2005, and they have not won one against a side other than Bangladesh since surprising India at Harare in 2001. In recent times, the Zimbabwean cricket community has watched in astonishment as their academy in Harare was burned down and then suffered the even greater indignity of being mocked by Ronnie Irani in a speech to the Cricket Writers' Club in 2007. Irani claimed that the Zimbabwean national anthem was 'Old MacDonald used to have a farm.' Zimbabwe used to have a cricket team worthy of the name too.

3

THE TACTICS

OF ALL stereotypes about cricket, one of the most frequently repeated is that cricket is played in the head as much as it is out in the middle. And it is true that mind games are everywhere. In real life we play them all the time, poking and prodding away in search of an Achilles heel to kick, an ego to flatter, a wound to reopen. In cricket the mind games can be crippling. And since it's such a perverse, don't-think-of-a-pink-elephant-gah-too-late! kind of a sport, you inevitably end up playing the games on yourself as much as on the opposition. Anyone who has ever taken part in so much as a beer match will know the paralysing inevitability of the moment the Doubts Start Creeping In.

Your team is batting first against a side who beat you the previous year and you're due in at No. 6. So far, so bearable. But hang on, who's that opening bowler with the foaming mouth and the other-worldly eyes? And why is he pawing at the turf and being restrained by his team-mates in his follow-through? Don't remember him from last summer's nine-wicket mauling. Why does our opening batsman – the only player in the team who is averaging in double figures this summer – keep patting the pitch down between deliveries? Bugger. No more patting for him. Clean-bowled playing no stroke. Must have done a bit. And there goes another. Better start warming up. Hope the opening bowlers are off by the time I get in. Would be lovely to get off the mark against the geriatric trundler rather than the wild man from the high veld who hasn't been fed for several days. Time for a few throw-downs. Bat and pad together. Move those feet. Watch the ball out of the hand. Nothing premeditated. Shit, another wicket. Looks like it kept low. If this were a county game it would have been called off by now, surely. You can't play on that. Hey? What? I'm in? Keep my seat warm. Back soon.

Pathetic, I know. But unless your name is Sir Isaac Vivian Alexander Richards, the chances are you do not walk out to the crease every time as if you own the ground and several of the buildings around it. No, you look for things that can go wrong to establish a cunning no-lose situation. It goes something like this: if and when things do go belly up (and we're talking Mike Gatting's belly here rather than Bruce Reid's) you can tut sadly and demoralise team spirit even further by saying you knew that nasty ridge just outside off-stump was going to render the lunatic from Bloemfontein unplayable. And if by some miracle everything goes swimmingly, well, you have – in your own all-too-easily-upset mind at least – triumphed over adversity and moved effortlessly from the realm of the gamma male to the beta minus. It is a defence mechanism, and we all do it. It's just that some do it better than others.

Several months before Michael Vaughan led England to Ashes success in 2005, I asked him how hard it would be to break a cycle of defeats that stretched back to 1989, the year civilisation as we know it ended. 'First and foremost,' he said, 'Australia are probably the best Test team that's ever lived, so there's no disgrace in losing to them. The only disgrace is if you don't compete.' It was a clever way to begin an answer. It respectfully acknowledged the excellence of the Australians in a manner that made the prospect of defeat completely understandable. At the same time it laid down a challenge for his own side. It was hard-nosed realism disguised as a battle cry. After England beat Australia, Vaughan claimed he had deliberately played down his side's chances in advance because the role of quietly confident underdog is the one all teams cherish. He did it brilliantly.

The tactic can work a treat at a less exalted level too. When Steve James turned up for Glamorgan's county championship game against Sussex at Colwyn Bay in 2000, he took one look at the pitch and told a BBC journalist: 'It would be nice to have a bowl on there. It's sure to dart around.' So when Sussex won the toss and elected to bowl, James had a ready-made excuse. At stumps, Glamorgan had reached 457 for 1, with James unbeaten on 193. He went on to make an undefeated 309 before Glamorgan declared on 718 for 3, which is the kind of total most of us only encounter when we have cheated at pencil cricket. And although James might genuinely have believed the pitch was ripe for the bowlers' exploitation, his tendency to downplay had helped lower his own expectations, and thus the pressure. More importantly, he ended up with a score that still forms a proud part of his email address (and beats lawrencebooth61@etc.com any day of the week).

So how much did Vaughan, who as a captain has to draw on the little grey cells more regularly than his team-mates, feel cricket was played in the mind? His answer was 70 to 80 per cent, which is infuriating to us lesser mortals who know this figure is based on the assumption that any old idiot can go inside-out to hit Shane Warne from leg-stump through extra-cover. But the more you think about it, the more it makes sense. After all, how much time does a top-class batsman actually spend physically scoring his runs? And how much time does he spend lolling on his bat at the non-striker's end, watching his partner turn white at the prospect of another bouncer from Brett Lee and catching the eye of the comely brunette in row F? (Having said that, Len Hutton had a theory that if a batsman under pressure had a white face he would be OK. It was the panicky red version that betrayed impending doom.) At least cricket fans listening to the Test at home on the radio can make a cup of tea between overs or kick the cat. The non-striker has no such luxury. So what does he do to get the most out of the 70 to 80 per cent Vaughan mentioned?

It seemed an obvious question to put to a sports psychologist. In the old days, these people would have been treated like witches and dunked in the local pond, the better to dissuade them from their hocus-pocus. Now, they are still regarded with suspicion in the less sophisticated parts of the cricketing world but increasingly embraced in more forward-thinking regions.

Market Harborough in the east Midlands does not sound like the most obvious place to go for enlightenment, but that's the home of Jeremy Snape, who played ten one-day internationals for England before taking a Masters in Sports Psychology at Loughborough University, setting up his own company, Sporting Edge Solutions, in 2005, and then being selected for England's fifteen-man squad to take part in the inaugural Twenty20 world championship in South Africa in September 2007. He was even part of the coaching team that helped Rajasthan Royals win the Indian Premier League in 2008. He lives and breathes sporting psychology, which made the question of con-centration at the crease something of a slow full-toss. 'Cricket is about turning the volume up and down,' he told me. 'People tend to say "switch on and switch off", but that's not entirely true, because you never switch off from it. It's more of a volume control in terms of your concentration and your focus. There was a famous line about Michael Atherton's innings of 185 not out in Johannesburg. He batted for eleven hours or something, and he said he'd only really batted for four – it wasn't anywhere near the time he'd been at the crease. He was able to switch from high-intensity focus at the moment of delivery to things like the crowd between balls. A lot of batsmen's success is down to the efficiency with which they do that.'

Sounds great. But how *do* you do it? How *do* you prevent the peripherals getting in the way? Looking back on my less-than-glamorous career as a medium-pace all-rounder, there have been countless examples of the mind messing it all up at the last second. The feeblest of my many weaknesses as a batsman – the runt of a particularly unhealthy litter – has been my tendency to play across the line to a full-length delivery for no reason other than I fancied clipping the ball through midwicket like those players on the telly. I know it is wrong, and talk to myself, like a younger version of Derek Randall, on my way to the middle. 'Play straight, Booth. Nothing fancy now.' My good intentions usually last about five balls before the bowler drifts onto middle stump. Then my eyes light up and my desire to look like Viv Richards takes over. Leg before wicket is my most common mode of dismissal. I fondly imagine my foible is a less elegant version of David Gower's off-stump fiddle. In other words, I feel powerless to stop it.

Funny things can happen with the ball too. Towards

the end of the same match in which I dispensed useful advice to Ian Bishop, the opposition needed seven to win with three wickets in hand. I had just sent down four reasonably tidy overs, but our opening bowler, the broadcaster Ralph Dellor, was desperate for a chance to have a crack at the tail and a tilt at glory. In a touchingly misplaced show of faith, the captain threw me the ball once more. 'I'll be fine,' I insisted as my palms began to ooze sweat and my left eye twitched uncontrollably. My first ball was a leg-side beamer that screamed away for five wides. Heads dropped. I could hear the collective groan, quiet but audible because eleven men had made it simultaneously: my ten team-mates plus one of the umpires, a fellow cricket journalist who always stood in our games and was, shall we say, a reassuring presence if you happened to be batting. Encouraged by this demonstration of unity, I served up a leg-stump half-volley which was clipped to fine-leg for four. I wouldn't say Ralph was looking smug, but then I wouldn't say he was looking distraught either. Like a South African in a semi-final, I had bottled it good and proper.

What is to be done to dismiss the gremlins and prevent the mind from running riot? The former Australia opener and coach Bobby Simpson used to talk his way out of a bad run with the bat by telling himself that he was still a good batsman and that a few low scores meant a big one must be round the corner. This is all well and good for a player who once hit an Ashes triple century, but at the time of writing my top score is 61 (see that unimpressive email address), and I don't really expect to beat it. I have made two half-centuries. Ever. After that, we're talking about a handful of unbeaten 20s. If a big score is round the corner, then it must be one of those corners in a drawing by Escher that never seems to end.

For Jamie Edwards, the answer in the case of Andrew Flintoff in 2005 was to work on his presence. 'Eldrick Woods becomes Tiger when he goes out to play,' he told Peter Hayter in *Ashes Victory*, the England team's official account of the series. 'Michael Jordan becomes Air Jordan. We needed to turn Andrew Flintoff into Freddie Flintoff. He has a warrior presence and a warrior doesn't walk into the arena with his head down.'

Again, this has a nice ring to it, but it is predicated on the notion of 'presence'. My arrival at the crease is usually greeted with titters at best, rank indifference at worst: Lawrence Booth becomes, well, Lawrence Booth. I suspect Snape's answer is more attainable for the average club cricketer, if only because it stresses routine rather than memories of your most recent Test hundred. The aim, he says, is to reach a state of unconscious competence – bear with me – whereby instinct takes over and puts into practice all those good habits you should have been acquiring in the nets.

Snape uses the analogy of learning to drive a car. 'There are four steps,' he says. 'Before I start learning how to drive, I have no idea how to do it: I am unconsciously incompetent. Then I become consciously incompetent: I sit in the car in Tesco's car park and realise I am crap. Then I become consciously competent: my dad is sitting with me, telling me to push that and move the gear here. I can do it. The mastery stage is unconscious competence, when you can do it without thinking about it. You get to fifth gear and sixth gear in your car, and you can't remember moving through third and fourth. The mastery of anything we do is done instinctively and without conscious thought.'

The so-called conscious-competence learning model is not a new one. While most psychologists agree it has been around as a formal notion since the 1970s, there are suggestions its basis can be traced back to the days of Confucius and Socrates, when even the concept of reverse swing was little more than a mystery. More recently, the cerebral Australian batsman Dirk Wellham lamented that the 'deplorable irony of batting is that once you think you should be aggressive, that instinctive aggression is tempered. Batsmen who do best are those who are relaxed, focused and not distracted by thought.'

What is new, however, is Snape's application of the idea to cricket, a sport in which – by his own tongue-in-cheek admission – reading material in the dressing room occasionally fails to stretch beyond the *Beano*. 'In cricket the time between deliveries will always make us aware of a conscious outcome,' he explains. 'Thoughts like, "This is the run-rate. This is where the fielders are. This bowler is trying to do this. The ball's new. It's going to bounce more. This wicket's dodgy. That last one kept low. I haven't scored a run. I never get runs at this ground." They're all conscious thoughts that stop the batsman playing at his best. So what we need to do is allow players to be instinctive.

'If you speak to most batsmen, their best pull shot is when they weren't even looking to pull the ball. The key is thousands of repetitions in the nets so that it becomes ingrained in your muscle memory. The only thing we need to do to trigger that instinctive shot is to see the stimulus, which is to see the ball come out at a certain length. What we do when we're consciously thinking and stirring up all the things that happened before and thinking about the consequences of not playing that shot, is that we cloud that, we stop that instinct from playing.'

Snape's approach echoes the findings of Dr Peter McLeod, who in 1986 carried out a series of tests at the Department of Experimental Psychology at Oxford University. Using Peter Willey, Allan Lamb, Wayne Larkins and John Lever as his guinea pigs, McLeod wanted to discover how top-class batsmen were able to react so adeptly in the face of a small round object hurtling towards them in excess of 90 mph. One of his conclusions, as outlined by Tony Francis in *The Zen of Cricket*, was that professional cricketers had the edge over their amateur counterparts mainly because repetition had turned their reflexes into second nature. 'It's conceivable,' said McLeod, 'that after years of highly motivated practice the flight of the ball becomes such a predictable and salient stimulus for professional cricketers that it can be handled like information about their own body rather than information from the outside world.'

It is another way of saying that you have to get into a state of mind where analysis gives way to instinct. And this, says Snape, is where cues or triggers come in. Watch top-class batsmen and most of them will have a routine before each delivery. Some are simple: Nick Knight used to touch the peak of his helmet like a village postman; Alec Stewart would twirl his bat as if he were a baton-wielding majorette. Others verge on the realm of obsessive-compulsive: Dermot Reeve seemed to adjust every part of his equipment, with special attention – the Freudians among you will note – paid to his box. The Hampshire wicketkeeper Nic Pothas carries out a series of strange gestures which seem to be based on measuring the distance from one imaginary spot to another. But however certifiable the cue, each has the same goal: to transport the batsman from the analytical to the instinctive without the panic that might otherwise arise in between.

Naturally enough, the fielding side takes great delight in trying to provoke this panic, by fair means or foul. One of Snape's greatest gifts to the game was the moon ball, an off-break tossed so high that it could easily have been confused with a celestial object. But the other possible etymology works just as well: the moon ball is in the air for so long that it would probably give the bowler enough time to bare his bottom and still take a return catch. Snape used it to great effect while Leicestershire were winning the Twenty20 Cup in 2004 and 2006, and believes it is a good example of staying one step ahead of the batsman. 'It's important not to be too caged in by tradition,' he says. 'A traditional off-spinner should look to flight the ball at 55 mph in a beautiful parabola just going outside off-stump and hitting middle. But if I do that in Twenty20 cricket, I'm dust. So you've got to find something else. And what I quickly worked out was that the best ball in Twenty20 cricket is the opposite of what the batsman's thinking. So if he's going to sweep me and he's predetermining the sweep shot, I've got to understand that.'

Staying one step ahead can be taken literally too. 'Preparation is everything for the bowler, and the batsman is the same,' says Snape. 'His preparation phase is me picking the ball up next to the umpire and walking back to my mark. If I go back 10 metres, get my fingers right on the ball, spin it up a few times, scratch my bum, look round at the crowd, do my hair and come in, he's got enough time to have a very clear thought about what he's going to do. So why don't I just stand next to the umpire and bowl? I don't need any run-up to bowl at my pace, and my action's strong enough to bowl off a yard. So where's his thinking time gone? He hasn't got any. So what's he more likely to do? Make a clouded judgement. Clouded judgements make you get out, make you choose the wrong options. The more he does that, the more times I win. If you analysed the balls that I bowled, I was one of the worst bowlers in county cricket. But the thinking isn't.'

In another move that is certain to outrage the purists who regard Twenty20 as the bastard offspring of international cricket's grubby alliance with the marketing men, Snape explains how it might not be such a bad idea to actually offer the batsman a single. Yes, that's *offer* the batsman a single. 'If the guy's a good player, he's a threat. So I think, I'm going to give him one: a full-toss on leg-stump to get him off strike. Now, how many bowlers in one-day cricket have given the bloke a run? But I know that when I bowl at the youngster at the other end and I bring the field in and change the pace at which I'm bowling, he doesn't play a big shot, so I can bowl a few dots to him, and I've gone for not very many off the over.' And if you think that's just talk, Snape's economy rate in the 2006 competition was a shade over six. Since a run a ball over the course of an innings gives you a total of 120 and the average first-innings score that year was roughly 50 more than that, this was pretty outstanding.

He has retired now, but when Snape first played county cricket for Northamptonshire in 1992, he learned about the game over a beer in the bar with the likes of Allan Lamb, Curtly Ambrose, Rob Bailey and David Capel.

But the onset of professionalism – showers these days are more likely to come in the form of water than Foster's lager – and the fashion for ice baths, rub-downs and early nights have led to less time for picking each other's brains. Snape says all he is doing is filling a gap left by the demise of the end-of-play refresher, even if he has to be careful not to cause players' eyes to glaze over with too much talk of unconscious incompetence. If it weren't for the bewildering number of syllables, unconscious incompetence sounds like precisely the sort of insult Merv Hughes might have hurled at Graeme Hick during the 1993 Ashes series. And underpinning everything Snape says is the matter of how to deal with sledging, a subject matter whose obvious appeal to fans keen to get inside the players' minds has spawned tomes and after-dinner speeches in their hundreds, not to mention the bulk of another chapter later in this book.

Snape says that self-confidence is a vital part of coping with Australian abuse, although he doesn't say whether this applies to life outside cricket as well. But for anyone who has been heckled with the line 'here comes the night-watchman' as they walk out to bat at No. 3 in the baking heat of the lunchtime sun – as I might once have been – the question still remains: how do you block out the barking and prevent it from chipping away at the protective layer which enables you to believe that you really are about to score your maiden hundred? Reassuringly, it has happened to the very best of us, since even Don Bradman may once have fallen victim to a bowler's taunts. Batting rather slowly at Adelaide against the gentlemanly Gubby Allen, the man who refused to follow Douglas Jardine's instructions and bowl Bodyline, Bradman was confronted with the not-exactly-withering: 'Why don't you have a go at 'em – they won't give you out!' He nicked the next ball into his stumps. According to Snape, the key to ignoring the claptrap lies, once more, in those cues: the tics and foibles which help ease any batsman into the frame of mind where only a chemical synapse separates you from that Mark Waugh-like cover-drive.

In some cases, the tics and foibles become ends in themselves. Mark Lathwell was a gloriously gifted opener for Somerset in the early 1990s, but he developed a pathological hatred of the spotlight. 'Publicity bothers me,' he told the *Guardian* journalist David Foot in 1993, the year of his brief elevation to the England side. 'I simply can't see why anyone should be interested in me. Maybe I'm subconsciously trying to slow it down. I want to avoid any impression that I'm more important than I am.' Walking out to open the innings against Australia at Headingley that year, he was told by his partner Mike Atherton: 'Good luck, the crowd are rooting for you.' Lathwell's reply was a masterpiece of self-defeating negativity: 'They won't be in a minute when I'm on my way back.' Foot would later write: 'Only the unimaginative players escape the tension. Many, whatever their seeming unconcern, retreat into caverns of introspection.' That day at Headingley Lathwell made a duck.

South Africa's Daryll Cullinan became so fearful of his encounters with Shane Warne that he sought out a psychotherapist for advice. As Warne put it with typical delicacy in his autobiography: 'I knew that Daryll was a bit fragile at times, but never imagined he would go to a shrink to learn how to read the googly.' In fact, the googly was low down the list of Cullinan's problems, beneath the

leg-break, the flipper, the slider, the zooter and presumably – as David Lloyd put it years later – the 'this-er and
the that-er'. As Cullinan took guard in Melbourne in 1997
for his first innings after his consultation, Warne was
standing there, tossing the ball from one hand to the other
like a coordinated praying mantis. 'Daryll,' he crowed, 'I've
waited so long for this moment and I'm going to send you
straight back to that leather couch.' The entry on the
scorecard reads 'Cullinan b Warne 0'. The situation
became so one-sided – Warne would eventually dismiss
Cullinan twelve times in international cricket – that before
the next Test at Sydney two senior members of the South
African side approached Warne and his captain Mark
Taylor to ask them to go easy on the verbals with Cullinan.
It must have been like telling Warne he couldn't eat pizza
for a year or text anyone on his mobile phone.

Appearances, then, can be everything. Snape chuckles
at the memory of his part in England's one-day tour of
India in 2002. 'I was in a press conference and a *Hindustan
Times* reporter said to me: "They tell us in India you're a
specialist one-day spin bowler. You must have a very clear
plan of how you aim to tame the tiger Tendulkar." I looked
at him and nearly laughed. But I had to say, "I've got some
plans but I'd like to keep them to myself at this stage."
Actually, I hadn't got a clue.' It is the modern-day equivalent of the Wilfred Rhodes observation about pitches
that may or may not be turning: 'If the batsman thinks it's
spinnin', it's spinnin'.'

The truth is that psychology, even reverse psychology,
has been around in one form or another in cricket since
the days when W.G. Grace tried to curb the big-hitting
instincts of the 6 ft 6 in Australian George Bonnor by

calling him – cover your eyes now – a 'slogger'. To Grace's delight, Bonnor responded by blocking, only for the Australia captain Billy Murdoch to drop him down the order, saying 'You are now only a plodder.' Bonnor responded in turn by begging to return to his normal batting berth, and promptly hammered the bowling all over the place just like old times. Then there's the time Australia's 22-year-old batsman Dirk Wellham was nearing a century on Test debut at The Oval in 1981. It was the fourth evening and England, who were up against it, did not want to bat before the close. As Wellham edged through the nineties, Ian Botham urged him on. 'Don't give it away now, Dirk. You've done all the hard work, Dirk. Just a few more runs, Dirk.' Wellham got his head down and spent twenty-five minutes on 99 before reaching three figures. His caution, thanks in part to Botham's cunning, meant Australia were unable to declare that night, and England finished the final day seven wickets down. QED.

England's captain that year was Mike Brearley, who tells a nice story in his mini-epic *The Art of Captaincy* about Derek Randall, an England colleague who on this occasion was playing in a county match for Nottinghamshire against Brearley's Middlesex. Randall was a hopelessly nervy starter, and the morning after he and Brearley had discussed the very topic, he hooked his second ball straight to Phil Edmonds at deep square-leg. Brearley then spent the night before Randall's second innings at Randall's house, and teased him on the way into the ground the next day about which ball the bouncer would be. Again, it was the second one. Again, Randall was caught on the boundary to complete one of the game's most glorious pairs.

The tale backs up one of Snape's more surprising contentions. 'I wasn't a great cricketer, but I'd say I was probably dismissed [by the skill of the bowler] ten times in my whole career. I'd hate to think how many times I got out, but it was a lot more than ten. There were thousands of times where I just thought the wrong thing at the wrong moment, or tried to play a too high-risk shot, or he's moved so I'll try to hit it there, or this bloke's going to bowl a good ball in a minute. Well, if you think that, you're out. It wasn't a good ball: you *made* it into a good ball.'

I once played in a friendly match for *Wisden* – the other matches in my career have, naturally, all been life-or-death affairs – against a team led by a wily 50-year-old who bowled that brand of darting off-spin which was the basis of John Emburey's entire Test career. Honed, presumably, through years of trying to keep youngish whippersnappers like myself quiet and driven by the obsessive desire not to give away a *single run as if his mortgage depended on it*, he would nag away like a broken tap. In case this gives the impression of permanence at the crease, I should add that I hit the old codger for a single boundary. And, yes, it was with a turn of the wrists through square-leg. 'He's aiming everything to leg,' he declared with enough venom and volume to suggest that he was personally affronted by my decision not to score exclusively on the off-side. But – and I write this with a hanging head, so please excuse any typing errors – the tactic worked. In the next over I tried to hit their left-arm seamer straight back past him and lost my middle stump. I glanced over at C. Odger esq., but he was already plotting the downfall of our next batsman. Outpsyched *and* ignored. It was quite a double.

To move from the ridiculous to the slightly less so, Don Bradman used to say that he never even considered the possibility of getting out. That's all very well if you spent your childhood hitting a golf ball against a water tank with a stump, but he had a point. Steve James had an even simpler one when I asked him about batsmen allowing their concerns to affect their game. 'So many batsmen worry too much about their technical aspects,' he said. 'And a lot of players don't watch the ball. They just look in the general direction, because they're so busy worrying about technical issues. I didn't watch the ball properly for the first five years of my career, until someone – I think it was my Glamorgan team-mate Adrian Dale – asked me whether I was. I said, "Yeah, of course I do." But when I went away and thought about it, I knew I wasn't.'

I realise I have concentrated mainly on batsmen here, but then batsmen are the ones faced with the more taxing existential problem: one mistake, and they're a goner. Bowlers can make a whole host of errors and still end up with five wickets. Conversely, they can become over-whelmed by the knowledge that it is their job to place the ball in the business area of the pitch. The result is the yips, an affliction that more commonly affects golfers on the putting green or journalist with a round to buy. But generally bowlers are not subjected to attempts by batsmen to put them off. The obstacle, if there is one, comes purely from within. Scott Boswell, a jobbing seam bowler for Leicestershire, famously fell to pieces during the 2001 Cheltenham & Gloucester Trophy final against Somerset at Lord's. To the undisguised mirth of one or two of his team-mates, he bowled eight wides in his second over and was immediately removed from the attack. Reduced to a gibbering wreck, he played his last game for the county a fortnight later, when the single over he sent down cost 18 runs. Boswell had forgotten how to do what should have come naturally to him.

Of course, there is another way of dealing with nerves, and it inhabits the opposite end of the mental spectrum from psychology. Richard Dawkins calls it the God Delusion, but I wonder whether he might question his ultra-atheism if his job as Oxford University's Professor of the Public Understanding of Science depended on him keeping out an over of leg-breaks and googlies from Mushtaq Ahmed. The role of religion in English cricket was never more explicit than when Sussex won the county championship in 2006 – their second triumph in four seasons – and their captain, Chris Adams, publicly thanked Allah for His contribution to their success. Adams was referring to Mushtaq's Muslim faith which, according to Mushy himself, helped him take 102 championship wickets that season at under 20 apiece. It might irk some to see Christian sportsmen crossing themselves or Muslims, such as Mohammad Yousuf, a convert from Christianity, kissing the ground. After all, why should God/Allah/Richie Benaud care about a batsman's average or a bowler's strike rate? But when I went to visit Mushtaq in his Brighton home in 2006, I was struck by the extent to which belief in the Almighty can be as useful to a cricketer as belief in unconscious competence.

'I ask God to help me and pray five times a day, and that helps me become a calm person and not worry about the results,' said Mushtaq. 'Since I've been into religion, it has helped my game big time. As a sportsman, it helps to remind you that your personality will be the same if you get five wickets or none for 200. It's about the bigger picture. I'm happy I can run, I'm happy I've got two arms, I'm happy I can see, and talk. I remember these things rather than what will happen if I don't bowl well tomorrow and we lose, and all the expectation on my shoulders and how I'm going to let people down. With religion, your personality stays very stable because God gives you coolness and calmness. He allows you to stay the same and not worry about the result.'

If, like Dawkins, you regard this kind of thinking as an insult to evidence-based rationality, then you are probably seething at the suggestion that Allah was instrumental in Sussex's success. But if one of the benefits of a belief in God is to maintain a perspective – one that allows you to see cricket for what it is – then you will agree that Mushtaq might just be on to something. It doesn't matter whether Mushtaq is right or wrong about the existence of Allah. What matters is that he *believes* he is right: and it is that belief which is the source of his strength. It is a more profound kind of psychology – with the added bonus of being relevant once the cricket is over for the day. And possibly to the after-life too.

In fact Mushtaq, in the years before he turned to Islam, was also open to the idea of a more secular approach to the psychology of sport. He told me about the time Pakistan were sorting out their game plan for the 1992 World Cup final against England. They had made a shocking start to the tournament and would have been knocked out if rain had not intervened after England had dismissed them for 74 at Adelaide. But their captain, Imran Khan, had exhorted his side to 'fight like cornered tigers' (the kind of instruction that would have been met with strange looks in a county dressing room), and now he worked his magic on his No. 1 leg-spinner.

'In the meeting we discussed Graeme Hick,' says Mushtaq. 'He was the in-form batsman. He was dangerous and everyone was worried about him because he can smash you any time. Imran Khan said to me in the meeting, "Mushy, if Graeme Hick comes to the crease, you make sure you bowl to him." I said, "Hang on, the guy who has been the cleanest hitter of the ball – and he can hit a long way – and I'm bowling to him!" But the way Imran said it, I could see the passion in his eyes. He was telling me I was the guy who's responsible to get him out. That makes my imagination go! Before the World Cup final I was imagining getting him out. I'm lying down in my hotel room, imagining if I bowl two leg-breaks, then I bowl a straight one, then I bowl a wrong 'un, maybe he can try to play a drive and go through the gate and I can bowl him and we can win the World Cup. And it happened. It was the highlight of my career.'

Back, one last time, to Snape. 'I did an interview with Glenn McGrath that I show in my consultancy. I started off by saying, "So you don't use a sports psychologist", and he said, "No mate, that's bullshit." For the next twenty minutes he told me everything about his elite performance, and it was all deeply seated in sports psychology. It was fascinating, and he came out with a quote: "The transition from first-class to international cricket is 90–100 per cent mental." The interesting thing for me was that one day I was playing for the Gloucester team and we were doing quite well. We'd get a few spectators in and I'd do OK and that's great. And the next month you're playing in front of 120,000 in India. No one's given me a magic stick and said, "There you go, there's all your wealth of talent and experience, go out and enjoy yourself." I'm the same bloke who was bowling at a cone in the indoor nets in Bristol when it was pissing down with rain two weeks ago to try to simulate the atmosphere.'

The answer, though it pains me to say it, lies within. And it lies in the ability to empty the mind of all bar the essential. George Headley once told C.L.R. James: 'When I am walking down the pavilion steps, going in to bat, if I met my father I wouldn't recognise him. And once I am at the wicket I am concerned with nothing else but seeing the ball from the bowler's hand . . .' David Steele told Tony Francis that the secret of his success against the 1975 Australians was that 'Once I took guard I was in a world of my own. It's the best I've ever felt mentally. Time didn't mean anything.' And in case you think this is a case of a cricketer talking out of his backside, here's the answer Pete Sampras gave to a journalist who asked him what was going through his mind when he closed out the 1999 Wimbledon final with a second-serve ace against Andre Agassi: 'There was absolutely nothing going through my mind.' Sometimes the truth can be tediously simple. But then sport contains more rudimentary emotions than people care to admit, especially when England are playing Australia . . .

4

THE PASSION

THE SUMMER of 2005 was less serene than you might imagine. Press boxes can be frantic places, especially when a fresh batch of cream buns arrives, but for sheer tension – of the kind felt by all sports journalists when they find their impartiality compromised by a strange desire for one team, say England, to thrash the living daylights out of the other, say Australia – nothing compared with the Ashes. No one came close to fisticuffs, but at times, as the cricket pushed supposedly grown adults to breaking point, it wasn't for want of trying. The snap, crackle and pop that resounded throughout the series was, of course, rooted in the centuries-old repartee between the English and the Australians, two nations, it has been pointed out often enough, separated by a common sport.

Robert Menzies, the Australian premier who adorned the walls of his prime-ministerial office with a photo of Keith Miller playing a square-cut, once said: 'Great Britain and Australia are of the same blood and allegiance and history and instinctive mental processes [Menzies came before Steve Waugh]. We know each other so well that, thank heavens, we don't have to be too tactful with each other.' Coming from an unreconstructed convict (just kidding), it was an eloquent point: plenty of four-letter words have been exchanged between Poms and Aussies over the years, but 'tact' is not high on the list. Indeed, watching them play cricket can spawn several neologisms that might struggle to make the *Oxford English Dictionary*. In 2005, one Australian journalist in particular really began to irk.

He worked in television, but never seemed to do much more than sit around during the day advertising his allegiance to anyone unlucky enough to be within earshot. (You might ask how his existence differed from that of the pressmen; it would be a fair point.) This journalist – let's call him Alf: something about him called to mind Alf Stewart from the Australian soap *Home and Away* – had advertised his green-and-goldness at the press conference that greeted Ricky Ponting and his men. 'Ricky,' he began, with a resonant 'R' that spelled trouble. 'The British tabloids are sure to beat up the line about Dad's Army. Are you concerned your side is too old?' Ponting smirked, possibly in appreciation at the gentle loosener. 'We weren't too old last time we played.' It was an innocuous enough answer, but Alf grinned as if Spike Milligan himself had just recounted the best joke in the world ever. This man would have to be watched.

It turned out he was tricky to ignore. He seemed to pop up at every press conference to ask the increasingly grim-faced Ponting whether he was 'dirty' about the latest injustice committed against his team by the umpires. The truth, of course, was that Alf was dirty himself. In fact, he was filthy, covered from head to toe in outrage at what he believed was little less than a conspiracy to wrench the Ashes from Australia's grasp. Due to a lack of space in the bomb shelter I was forced to sit next to him during the fourth Test at Trent Bridge. Steam was already coming out of his ears, because Australia had been forced to follow on for the first time in a Test since 1643 or thereabouts. Then Justin Langer gloved Ashley Giles to Ian Bell at short-leg and practically gave himself out. A replay appeared on the TV screen in the far corner of the press box. 'Nowhere near it!' bellowed an apoplectic Alf, rage seeping from every orifice. 'You've got good eyesight,' I said, beginning to steam up myself. Later, in the press conference, Langer admitted he had 'hit the cover off it'. I glanced around the room to see if the admission in any way changed Alf's world view, but he was nowhere to be seen. He was probably off collecting evidence to present to the UN.

If Alf had been a West Indian or a New Zealander or a Pakistani, I would barely have given two hoots about a perspective that made Long John Silver look two-eyed. But he was an Australian. And the Australians had had it their way for too long. If Damo or Punter or Binger or Pidge – those nicknames! – were going to suffer a bit of bad luck for once, I was not going to shed a tear. Hell, I shed plenty during the wilderness years that turned my adolescence and beyond into an unreasonable cauldron of anti-Aussieness: from 1989 onwards, Australia had won eight Ashes series out of eight, usually by thumping margins and always, it seemed, with a sadistic pleasure. For an Englishman of my generation, hope did not so much spring eternal as dribble briefly. The truth was I had joined the fray at precisely the wrong moment. I was vaguely aware of Mike Gatting's triumph in 1986–87 – let's face it, we all harked back to those golden few months often enough – but football was my sport back then and in any case the Australians were beaten almost as a matter of course in the 1980s. No, 2005 was the first time I had lived and breathed every ball of a *victorious* Ashes series, and I wasn't going to allow Alf or any other soap-opera lookalike to spoil it for me.

Of course, Alf and I were merely acting out roles that had been written for us over and over again. Once the

Ashes dust had settled – and with the disingenuous magnanimity of the victor – it was clear to me I bore him no grudge, or at least not one that would have stood up in court. It was also fairly clear that Australian journalists did not have the monopoly on chauvinism, as the English like to think. But there is something about an Ashes series that precludes rational judgement, especially if you have spent most of the previous fifteen years watching your side take one hell of a beating.

Before the most recent hell of a beating – the restoration of the status quo in 2006–07 – I spoke to Mark Taylor, who in spite of being a thoroughly nice man had captained Australia to three series wins in the 1990s. Drawing on all my skills as an investigative sleuth, I asked him what was special about the Ashes. 'It's the word itself,' he said. 'You hear it in rugby league, but it was born in Test-match cricket back in 1882. The fact that it was born in cricket makes it special and the players are aware of that.' While I wondered how many cricketers could pluck 1882 out of the bag, Taylor's gut reaction to a straightforward question was revealing. History matters, particularly to Australia. If the Ashes represents a drop in the chronological ocean for England, then the Australians have been playing the series for over half their westernised existence. I have never quite bought the old gag about the difference between yoghurt and Australia (one has more culture than the other), but it is true that sport comes as close as anything to defining the country. And cricket comes closest to being the country's national sport. In England cricket symbolises many different things, but the nation's well-being is not one of them.

No sport is prouder of its history than cricket, and in

that history no battle is more heavily chronicled than the Ashes. Ever since W.G. Grace ran out Sammy Jones at The Oval in 1882 after Jones had left his ground to tend to a divot – gamesmanship is not a recent invention – the two countries have been reluctant to give each other an inch. That Oval Test as we've seen, of course, was the game that gave birth to the legend of the Ashes, and when Ivo Bligh led his England team to Australia the following winter the legend was in full swing. So much so that Australia's fast bowler, Frederick 'The Demon' Spofforth – like Jason Gillespie but without the goatee, mullet or Test double century – is believed to have thrown a punch at Dick Barlow as the players left the field following England's series-clinching win at Sydney. Barlow's error had been to take 7 for 40 and skittle Australia for 83.

Yes, competition has always been of the no-holds-barred variety, but lurking not far from the front of this particular Pommie's mind is the fact that it has usually been settled in Australia's favour. Of the 222 Tests played between the sides since the First World War, Australia have won 96 to England's 57 – and that includes the morale-sapping 5–0 whitewash in 2006–07, another example of the elemental fury that lurks in Australian bellies whenever their sporting excellence is called into question.

Why the relative one-sidedness? Why, when England play out of their skins and the Australians are below par, is the score only 2–1 to England? And why, when the circumstances are reversed, is it 5–0 to Australia? The part played by the Ashes in the two nations' history may have something to do with it: you can sense the writing of a fresh page every time the Australians take the field. But so may a lot of other things. A few theorists have tried to explain the discrepancy by quoting a seductive line by the Australian philosopher David Stove. 'My own belief,' he wrote in his essay 'Cricket versus Republicanism', 'is that it is due to a difference in attitude towards the opponent: that whereas the Australians hate the Poms, the Poms only despise the Australians.' Stove's uplifting thesis strikes a chord without ringing completely true.

First, it overlooks the words of Douglas Jardine before the Bodyline series in 1932–33, when he supposedly told his team-mate Gubby Allen: 'We have to hate them. That's the only way we're going to beat them.' (Jardine insisted that any mention of Don Bradman, whose name was to the England captain what Macbeth is to actors, had to be replaced by the charming epithet 'the little bastard'.) Second, it relies on the idea that to hate is a more useful emotion in sport than to despise, which is surely more distant, less heated and thus arguably more capable of coming up with a scheme such as Jardine's Bodyline or the time-wasting talents of Trevor Bailey, who on a bright morning at Lord's once managed to avoid facing a final over before lunch at a crucial stage of an Ashes Test by appealing to the umpires against the light. By the time the umpires had considered his request, as they were obliged to do, the clock had ticked over to 1 p.m. and Bailey – butter incapable of melting in his mouth – was halfway back to the pavilion. Third, for all the silent seething between Alf and me, the two countries don't really hate or despise each other in the way that Indians and Pakistanis used to before relations thawed in 2003–04. They are in effect one and the same after all, the one merely the distance of a global-length umbilical cord away from the other. Degrees of antipathy have been the least of England's concerns, even when Jeff Thomson or Merv Hughes, whose idea of mixing it up meant a different oath every over, have been bowling.

I prefer to think of the difference between the two nations as being rooted in mild exasperation at the oddities of the other. When severe storms in January 2005 destroyed the iconic lime tree that stood inside the boundary of Kent's St Lawrence Ground (four runs if you hit it, even if the ball clips a twig on its way to an apparent six) the club had no hesitation in finding a replacement. The former Kent coach John Wright recalls the reaction of Dave Gilbert, an Australian fast bowler who went on to work in cricket administration: 'A tree gets in the way for two hundred years and, when it falls down, instead of cheering, they plant a new one.' Elsewhere, Gideon Haigh has not been alone in noting the failure of Australian lateral thinkers such as Bobby Simpson and John Buchanan to gain acceptance in the occasionally stubborn world of county cricket. After Simpson finished a coaching stint with Leicestershire, their captain James Whitaker was supposed to have complained: 'The big problem with Bob was that he wanted us all to be Test cricketers.' Simpson's response? 'Just fancy that!'

English attitudes to Australia, by contrast, tend to focus on the irritating fact that they are rather hard to beat, a galling state of affairs that can be softened by a damning pay-off line about Aussie officialdom. Thus Frank Tyson would tell the author Chris Westcott: 'Len Hutton always said to win in Australia you have to be 25 per cent better than they are, firstly because the conditions are foreign to you, and secondly you have to overcome disadvantages like the heat and sometimes rather ordinary umpiring.' And to think the Australians regard us as whingers.

As we suggested earlier sociologists will always argue that climate is a major factor in helping Australia maintain their edge. As any budding Shane Warne or Brett Lee will tell you, hot weather and hard pitches are more conducive to leg-spin and fast bowling – those two lethal weapons of the international game – than a spruced-up pudding at Derby. Peter Roebuck, the Englishman-turned-Australian, believes the differing climates have shaped diametrically opposed mentalities. 'Almost from the start,' he writes in *In It To Win It*, 'Australia's approach reflected the heat and dust of the interior, the baked ground and vast open spaces that encouraged boldness even as England's drizzle, mud and enclosed fields preached caution.' It's a broad-brushstrokes theory, but in a sense he is right: the sun *can* lift your mood and encourage the kind of risk-taking that might not call to mind Chris Tavare on one of his more cautious days.

Yes, the right attitude (or, as John Buchanan might have put it, 'the necessary psychological processing procedure'). Take 1989, a year the more religious of England supporters still keep at arm's length with a sign of the cross. Australia had lost three of the previous four Ashes series and their captain Allan Border, who had presided over disasters in 1985 and 1986–87, was getting sick of it. A smile in defeat, he decided, would be replaced by a snarl in victory. Not many gave him a chance, including – crucial, this – the England team. (Mind you, 'team' in the singular is a touch misleading: England picked 29 players that summer; only once before, in 1921, had they picked more. And still they lost 4–0.) And if the image of the series was of Merv Hughes wiping gobbets of spittle-flecked fury from his handlebar moustache, then the Aussies were also clever enough to say nothing out in the middle if they felt the batsman enjoyed a chinwag. 'Sorry, Lubo,' the usually loquacious fast bowler Geoff Lawson muttered to David Gower from mid-on. 'I'm not allowed to talk to you.' Still, it made a change from 'Up yours, ya Pommie bastard'.

Australian cricket was at one of its lowest ebbs in the mid-1980s; their response was to get off their lager-fattened behinds and do something about it. England had been living off the glories of Ian Botham's heroics in 1981, a performance that did not so much paper over the cracks as decorate them with gold leaf. Everything, we were tempted to assume, was fine. Yet when Mike Atherton became the twenty-third England cricketer to appear in that 1989 series, he remembered being told by one senior colleague that you play your first Test for love and the rest for money. Since several of his team-mates had already announced they would be travelling to apartheid-riven South Africa as part of a rebel tour, it seemed as if cynicism was a prerequisite to win an England cap. And the response to this crisis? 'I am not aware of any mistake I've made,' said the chairman of selectors, Ted Dexter, after rain had saved England in the sixth Test at The Oval. Unwittingly, Dexter was paving the way for years of misery.

The English tend not to be very good at admitting their errors. Yet if they had been even half as good as the Australians, they might not have needed to wait until 2005 for their next triumph. Here's Ian Chappell in 1998, at the height of Australia's dominance: 'There is still a "we rule the world" mentality in sections of [English] cricket. Consequently there's never been a full-throated admission that England is playing crap . . . Australia's honest and forthright admission served it well, while England's stiff-upper-lip approach has elongated the healing process.'

A year after Chappell's warning, England lost at home to New Zealand and plunged to the bottom of the Wisden world rankings, an outcome so humiliating that the *Sun* splashed 'RIP English Cricket' across its front page in an unusually erudite reference to the mock obituary that kicked off the whole contest back in 1882. When a tabloid cleared the decks of its usual diet of gossip, tits and football, you knew things must be bad.

These were not merely dark days for followers of the English game, they were character-forming. I grew up expecting England to lose to Australia; I developed a premature sense of world-weary ennui that may yet send me to an early grave. I even began to question other, completely irrelevant, aspects of Englishness. If the bus to school was late, well, it was an English bus, wasn't it? If my bike got a puncture it was patently because the tyre had not been manufactured in Australia. There were moments when it all became too much, when hope was cruelly allowed to linger only to be gobbled up by a squat, moustachioed Aussie and spat out like one of their interminable pieces of chewing gum. Did it get any worse than the second Test against Australia at Melbourne in 1990–91? England had built on a first-innings lead of 46 and were moving to 103 for 1 in their second innings, thanks to Graham Gooch and Wayne Larkins; (Larkins owed his place in the squad to the fact that he always seemed to score runs against Gooch's Essex on the day before the selectors met, but he was one of my idols all the same). Then, suddenly, as I listened in horror on my bedside radio to events on the other side of the globe, it was over: England 150 all out, Bruce Reid taking 7 for 51. The next day Australia recovered from 10 for 2 to win by eight gut-wrenching wickets.

Did it get any worse? God, yes. While inter-railing in Europe in my post-A-level summer of 1993, I learned that Australia had 653 for 4 declared at Headingley, a venue where Neil Mallender had run through the Pakistanis the previous year with his amiable medium-pace. The joys of Venice were lost amid the misery. But the killer blow came on 3 August 2001 at Trent Bridge, a game England needed to win to keep the Ashes alive (and how often had *that* clause been written in the preceding decade?). Shane Warne had removed Mike Atherton, unjustly given out caught behind, and Alec Stewart, justly bowled, in quick succession. But at 126 for 4 in their second innings, a lead of 121, England were still reasonably placed. Mark Ramprakash had battled hard for his 26 and there were nine overs of the second day to go. It was precisely the kind of 50–50 moment the Australians had been seizing with their eyes closed since 1989. Ramps, God bless him, was getting stuck in. My hope-ometer, a cruel piece of equipment that had exploded in my face so often over the years, was starting to splutter into life. Quite why Ramps then decided to charge down the wicket in an attempt to hit Warne into Nottingham city centre has always eluded me. Warne later claimed he goaded him into it, but then one of Warne's many talents was the ability to apply a retrospective sheen of Machiavellian genius to his dismissals. 'He loves his propaganda,' an England bowler would tell me years later. Anyway, with an early example of the twinkle toes that would one day win him fame on *Strictly*

Come Dancing, Ramps charged, missed, and was stumped by the length of the River Trent. I was working for *Wisden* at the time, where my job was to write regular updates of England's Tests for the company's new website. Yet instead of putting finger to keyboard, I slammed forehead on desk. 'Are you OK?' asked the managing editor. 'Gnnrrhhh,' I said. It was the point of no return. England lost the match comfortably and with it another series. They had tried to stare fate in the face and ended up squinting past its left ear. It was the story of my youth.

Until England surrendered at Adelaide in 2006–07, the Ramprakash stumping was my personal Ashes low point. But my personal *England* low point full stop had taken place several years earlier. I was following the tours of Zimbabwe and New Zealand from my student digs in Freiburg, Germany, where the hopelessness of the local football team and the perpetual fog that shrouded this lovely Black Forest town in the winter months did little to lift the gloom. Somehow, my tinpot radio managed to pick up live commentary of the Tests, and I can still remember contentedly switching it off in the very small hours when the New Zealand No. 10 Simon Doull was bowled by Darren Gough shortly after lunch on the last day. At that stage New Zealand led by virtually nothing, with only Danny Morrison to keep Nathan Astle company. Morrison had made twenty-four ducks in his Test career and had done well to keep the tally so low. It was game over. I nestled into my pillow.

Good old New Zealand, I mused in my half-slumber. England might have been bad in the 1990s, but the Kiwis were worse. I loved them. They always gave us a morale-boosting series victory just when we needed it. A great

bunch of guys and wonderfully accepting of their useless-
ness. A few hours later, I woke up and did what any self-
respecting cricket fan would do. I reached for the radio,
knowing that the sound of some doddery old brass band
dug up from the archives would mean the BBC were trying
to fill dead air time. It would mean England had won. 'And
Morrison plays that one back down the pitch to the
bowler,' said a voice. 'Sheesh, he's played well.' This was
not happening! The game was heading for a draw!
England had blown it! Morrison, one of the worst batsmen
in the history of cricket, would finish not out on 14 from
166 minutes and hands would be shaken! 'What's wrong?'
asked one of my German flatmates next morning.
'England drew with New Zealand,' I said, barely able to
look up from my Bircher muesli. He stared at me with
chilling indifference. If only C.B. Fry had successfully
persuaded Joachim von Ribbentrop, Hitler's foreign
minister, that the Germans should take up Test cricket, he
might have shared my pain.

But back to the English sporting fan's other great
nemesis. In part, I blame the baggy green, a vital symbol of
what it is to be Australian that doubles up as a link to the
past. Steve Waugh may have turned the baggy green into a
cult scary enough to merit police investigation, but then
you had to admire his ability to convince a whole
generation of Australian cricketers that it was far more
than a piece of embroidered green felt. Listen to this
frightening spiel from Justin Langer, known in some
circles as 'mini-Tugga' because of his devotion to all things
Waugh (Tugga Waugh: geddit?). 'You know what?' he
asked, knowing full well no one had the faintest idea. 'It's
not just a game to me. I've had the same cap for thirteen

years. It's the greatest game in the world. I love it, and I'll
be involved in it until my last breath. It's been a vehicle.
I've learned how to handle success, how to handle
criticism, how to handle failure, how to fight back from
adversity. I've learned about mateship, leadership. It's all
because of the baggy green cap.' To which there is only
one possible response: yikes! If an Englishman spoke with
the same ingenuous enthusiasm about the pride of wearing
the three lions, we would slap him round the face and tell
him to stop being hysterical. And that, perhaps, is half the
problem. 'After all,' wrote J.B. Priestley, the Yorkshire-born
novelist whose thought processes were sufficiently clear to
turn down a knighthood and a peerage, 'there are other
things than games, and England is not ruined just because
sinewy brown men from a distant colony sometimes hit a
ball oftener than our men do'.

Most Australians have no time for such intellec-
tualising. The baggy green helps their cricketers feel part
of a continuum, from Victor Trumper via Don Bradman to
Steve Waugh and Ricky Ponting. Today's players have all
heard about Clem Hill and Warwick Armstrong and Bill
Ponsford. Like Mark Taylor, they seem to know about the
significance of 1882. And that knowledge is a badge of
honour rather than a sign of geekery. It must also be a
source of strength, a reminder of a large family tree
(eucalyptus, naturally) whose roots reach back to the days
when the Poms were treated with a respect that bordered
on reverence. When, for example, England arrived down
under to unleash Harold Larwood, Bill Voce and Bodyline,
the Australian captain Bill Woodfull's innocent pre-series
speech made him sound suspiciously like the Harry Enfield
character Mr Cholmondeley-Warner: 'You have sent us a

great side. But, after all, that's just what we Australians expect from the home country. Win or lose, the motherland has always put up a strenuous fight.' Jardine thanked him by instructing his bowlers to bowl bouncers at leg-stump.

England's relationship with its past is more ambivalent. If players are not being weighed down by the pomp and circumstance of a stroll through the Long Room at Lord's, they are being berated by Geoff Boycott or Brian Close. The past, for them, is more of an albatross: history as encumbrance rather than inspiration. The need for a fresh start has informed too much of their cricket over the years. Put simply, the baggy green has always roared more effectively than the three lions.

Whether or not the Australians have simply produced more talented players – which is probably the case – they have always been the better side at drawing on their heritage. And heritage does not come much more inspirational than Don Bradman. Cowed by the prospect of following in the footsteps of sport's greatest phenomenon? Not the Australians, whose ethos of 'Have a go, yer mug' is as deeply ingrained in the culture as the lyrics of 'Waltzing Matilda'. When Ted Martin, a former leg-spinner for Western Australia, turned 100 in 2002, he joked: 'It's nice to have beaten Bradman at something.' Everyone in Australia knows Bradman died at 92. Cricket, Australia learned through the Don, was a way of getting one over the Poms and putting themselves on the map. It is a need the English, with their rich history, their seat at the high table of international politics, and their obsession with football, have never felt quite as strongly. If the English were once told by Cecil Rhodes that they had won first prize in the lottery of life, the Australians have been burdened with no such delusions of grandeur. Who cares whether no sane England player these days actually believes all the bull about a land of hope and glory? If the Australians can convince themselves that the English believe it, then they will always be able to rouse the chippy colonial within.

Perhaps they have always been the hungrier, more confident of the two people anyway. In his travel book *Australia and New Zealand*, written in 1873 – four years before the first ever Test at Melbourne – the English novelist Anthony Trollope noted the Australians' tendency to 'blow' about how wonderful their country was. This could, of course, be put down to insecurity, but then the *appearance* of confidence counts for so much in sport. And in any case, I haven't met too many insecure Australians. One hundred and thirty-three years later I was sitting in the press box at Perth feeling rather pleased that England had just dismissed Australia for 244 on the first day of the third Test, a game they needed to win – or at least not lose – if they were to etc etc. The journalists were separated from a boozy corporate function by a curtain, which kept the revellers out of sight, if not earshot. Then, between innings, a man poked his head through the partition. 'Enjoy it while it lasts,' he growled with a friendly glint in his eye. 'Because it won't last for long.' It was Terry Jenner, the leg-spinning guru who was always Shane Warne's first port of call if he needed to fine-tune the flipper, or christen another scary-sounding delivery to outpsych the Poms. The English journalists laughed nervously. Australia won the Test at a canter. Jenner knew it would happen, and so did we. So too, I expect, did both sides.

If Australians like to blow, it is usually because they

rarely look stupid after the event. And if blowing is a national pastime, then it probably derives from a healthy capacity for not beating about the bush. Australians are instinctively drawn towards the American model of equality; the English tendency to place everything in a hierarchy leaves them cold. After all, it was as recently as 1963 that English cricket finally abolished the distinction between the amateur Gentlemen and the professional Players. Australia's mateship ethic militates against such snobbery: during the Second World War, Australia's soldiers held captive by the Japanese were staggered at the British officers' refusal to help their men clear jungle and build bridges and railway lines. One prisoner noted that the Aussie officers seemed to have a lot more 'push and go' than their British counterparts. Decades later and the analogy still holds good: their international cricketers have much closer ties to the grass-roots game than the English, and their supporters feel less awed as a result. Michael Vaughan was struck how, on his first visit to Australia in 2002–03, he would turn round to find small boys tittering at him because he played for a team that kept losing. But this glorious lack of respect has always been there. Alec Bedser recalls being approached by a boy in Glenelg, near Adelaide. 'You've spoilt my weekend,' said the boy. 'I could hit you. Why did you bowl out Don Bradman for a duck?' When England's fans retaliated with some vicious gloating in 2005, it all seemed so out of character.

I was not the only one to shake my head in despair at the story of the England batsman who turned up for his Test debut in 2001 driving an open-topped sports car and wearing a pair of look-at-me shades. The story goes that Steve Waugh, sitting in the oh-so-democratic Australian team coach, spied this vision of premature self-congratulation and chuckled quietly. He knew that in Australia such ostentation would have been frowned upon if it had come from a veteran of 100 Tests; to see it in a debutant told him that nothing had changed: English cricketers still had a high opinion of themselves. In Australia, many of the best players – from Don Bradman to Glenn McGrath – worked their way up from humble beginnings. English newcomers who arrive at the ground behaving like *Big Brother* contestants do nothing to dispel the suspicion that they have lost a sense of perspective.

The meritocracy can be felt on the field too. Whereas Australia have usually chosen their captain only after choosing their best XI, England have preferred to get the hierarchy in place first. Whether or not this is a throwback to the days when England captains had 'Lord' before their name, such as Lord Harris, or 'Hon.', such as Ivo Bligh, Frank Jackson and Lionel Tennyson, is a moot point. But one thing is for sure: Chris Cowdrey would never have been appointed captain of Australia to take on the might of the West Indies in the 1980s. Cowdrey was the third England captain out of four who held the post in the shambolic summer of 1988. He hadn't played at the top level for three and a half years, and appeared to get the job largely by virtue of being the godson of Peter May, the chairman of selectors, who used to play for England with Cowdrey's more famous father, Colin. Cowdrey Jnr made 0 and 5, went wicketless and was dropped for good: his Test batting and bowling averages of 14 and 77 remain a low point in the history of nepotism. (Australia's cricket families, such as the Chappells and the Waughs, are by contrast of the highest calibre.) Sometimes the captain-first policy paid off: Mike Brearley remains the classic example. But towards the end of the 1980s, batsmen such as Mark Nicholas and Peter Roebuck were being mentioned as potential England leaders when neither was quite good enough as a batsman. This does not merely demonstrate the age-old English faith in the notion that your captain must be made of the right stuff, whatever that is. It is also an indulgence, and I suspect the Australians, who felt they were getting dangerously close to the English model when Mark Taylor was struggling to score a run in the mid-1990s, have always laughed about it.

For a while Nasser Hussain looked as if he might fall into the same trap. Not long after taking over the England captaincy from Alec Stewart in 1999 – one of his first deeds was to weep with shame on the Oval balcony after defeat to New Zealand – he entered a batting trough of nightmarish proportions: twenty-one Test innings and more than fourteen months with a top score of 51. Typical, we all tutted. England finally get a decent captain and he suddenly forgets which end of the bat to hold. Yet Hussain did what no England captain before him had done. He turned a cliché into a virtue by wearing his heart on his sleeve and fuming at aspects of Englishness that really bugged him. When Mike Gatting criticised Hussain – as he tended to on the slightest pretext – for saying that he would like to play 100 Tests for England, Hussain thundered: 'I'm not apologising for having ambitions. It's the English mentality. When someone states "I'm ambitious", he gets knocked. Here, everyone loves a loser.' It was no coincidence that under Hussain, aided though he undoubtedly was by the introduction of central contracts, England stopped playing like losers. They were no longer a laughing stock.

Or were they? Part of the curse of the contemporary English cricketer is the legacy handed to them on a not-very-silver plate. Encouraged by a fickle press, the public easily take refuge in old habits. And in cricketing terms that means laughing at the England team, those toffee-nosed fools who enliven our winters by losing in yet another corner of the old Empire. The public also pay next to no attention to games against teams other than Australia, which does not exactly help matters either. If England beat Australia, as in 2005 – have I mentioned that year already? – then everyone becomes a cricket fan. If England lose to Australia, like they do the rest of the time, the acolytes shrink to the hard core, and the jokes start all over again.

You might think that, as a cricket lover, I am especially sensitive to the mocking. And you would be right. But it is not a problem Australians, used to almost unbridled success over the years, have to deal with. It helps that cricket is the only truly national sport down under, even if it is run close by Pom-bashing and tasteless-lager-swilling. It also helps that Australia does not have the same tradition of self-mockery, although mocking others is another matter altogether. But then the perception of cricket is different in Australia, where the concept of the gentleman's game barely exists. Mention cricket in England, and Joe Public will immediately think of the Marylebone Cricket Club, cucumber sandwiches and village greens you could eat those same cucumber sandwiches off. No matter that recent England sides have been very short on the public schoolboys who used to run the game and invariably found themselves president of the MCC: preconceptions stick, and the knee-jerk preconception in England is that cricket is still ever so slightly class-ridden and more than slightly ridiculous.

The Scottish broadcaster and journalist Nicky Campbell summed up this particular strain of British anti-cricketness in his *Guardian* column. 'Sledging is one of the redeeming features of cricket,' he wrote. 'It reassures this agnostic that the game has a pulse and swipes Robin Williams' description of it as "baseball on Valium" into a cocked white panama hat. It also whacks that preposterously naff public school sense of fair play balderdash right out the ground. Ah yes, the two most reassuring sounds for an English gentleman – leather on willow and leather on buttocks. I suspect I share Merv [Hughes]'s opinion on that one.' Quite cute, but not really very helpful. The ground authorities at Brisbane's Gabba stadium had an equally unsubtle perspective on the English cricketer. To pass the time between overs and advertise a particular brand of mobile phone, the giant screen during the 2006 Ashes Test would invite spectators to answer a multiple-choice quiz question by sending a not-especially-cheap text message. Most of the questions concerning Australians focused on their superhuman derring-do. How many Test runs had Allan Border scored? How many pathetic Poms had Steve Waugh sledged? How many beers can David Boon get down his oversized torso in one hour? That sort of thing. But when the questions pertained to Englishmen, the tone changed. Which former England fast bowler wrote poetry in his spare time? (Answer: John Snow). Or: Which illness did the former England captain Wally Hammond suffer from? (Answer: syphilis). The implication was clear. The Poms were either effete bastards, or diseased bastards. And in neither case, it went without saying, did they take regular showers.

Traumatic experiences lead to coping mechanisms,

and over the years I have developed one of my own. The Australians, I decided early on, took sport too seriously. They had no perspective, because their own sense of self-worth was tied up with hitting a small leather ball and knocking down a few pieces of wood and doing it better than the other lot. Stupid game anyway. No, it was self-deprecation that counted, and to hell with the Ashes and its overblown history. Could you imagine a modern Australian raising an ironic glass of champagne to the fall of an English wicket, as David Gower did during the summer of 1989? And how ridiculous was Ricky Ponting's sour reaction to a taunting video message from Phil Tufnell at the annual Allan Border Medal night in 2006? Tufnell had been cheeky enough to interrupt what one Australian journalist described at the time as 'the ritual back-slapping and self-congratulation' to remind the locals of a few memories from the 2005 Ashes. His jibes were cheap but amusingly so. Tuffers pointed out that Glenn McGrath's batting average for the series had been higher than Adam Gilchrist's. He wondered whether Shane Warne needed to get counselling after dropping Kevin Pietersen at The Oval. And he reminded Ponting that he had inserted England at Edgbaston.

Ponting was not happy and said as much. And nor was the Australian journalist, only for different reasons. 'Sadly, the reaction to his comedy instead said more about the nation we're becoming,' he wrote. 'Triumphant in victory, precious, thin-skinned and defensive in defeat. One radio news bulletin described the light-hearted routine as a "spiteful send-up". Radio phone-ins lamented how such un-Australian sentiments could be uttered on this sacred night of nights. Tufnell could scarcely have caused more offence had he turned up to the Muslim Cricketer of the Year dinner with cartoons of Muhammad all over his napkin.' Yes, moments such as that have persuaded me in a none-too-convincing way that it was more desirable in the long term to lose regularly and graciously than rarely and bitterly. And the emotion sustains me for as long as it takes England's batsmen to collapse in another heap [insert your own gag here].

It's no good. Coping mechanisms are actually escape mechanisms. Perhaps the best way is to get your retaliation in first. The example of Darren Gough passing through Australian customs is salutary. Australian immigration's paranoia about foreigners bringing in deadly flora and fauna on the soles of their mud-caked boots has often meant England's cricketers spend the first few minutes of their trip having the gunge scraped off by uniformed Aussies. When Gough whipped out his social shoes and asked for a quick polish while they were at it, it was reportedly the only time in living memory the officials had been stunned into silence. Because the truth is that most Aussies regard banter as their lingua franca: they are far more likely to warm to you if you respond with a one-liner rather than a sulk.

On my first work-related trip to Australia in 2006–07 I was delighted when one of the local journalists said he would review a book I had recently written in his diary column. Next day, I began reading and was met with this opening line: 'It takes a while to warm to the English and Lawrence Booth . . . is no exception. Booth, like most of his countrymen, is a rather lugubrious lad who attempts to fashion a cheerful demeanour by wearing a range of pink polo shirts . . .' And so it went on, until its ringing conclusion: 'Anyway, *Arm-Ball to Zooter* is a nice colour and just the right size to stick in the s-bend of the sink which makes it rather perfect for the smallest room in the house.' At this stage of the tour England were 3–0 down, and the article did not improve the mood of some of my colleagues. I resolutely refused to take offence: the journalist had become – in the best Australian traditions – a 'mate'. I was even prepared to overlook the libel about the polo shirts. Even so, a couple of weeks later a guilt-ridden email landed in my inbox. The Aussie journalist spent a meaty paragraph reassuring me that, in fact, he loved the book and finished with the line: 'Don't they realise we only take the piss out of people we like?' As a summary of the Anglo–Australian dynamic, it was perfect.

5

THE SHAME

YOU WILL have gathered by now that, against my better judgement, I feel quite strongly about cricket. Oh, what the hell, I love it. And it is a love that by and large dares speak its name, unless I am stuck on the District Line with a bunch of drunken Chelsea fans, at which point we all agree that cricket is a pastime for chinless inbreds. Yet, like most loves, this one is never more than the width of an ICC Code of Conduct report away from irritation. Imagine your grandpa constantly harking back to the halcyon days when men were men, fields Elysian, and Bob Willis was not in a trance. Then notice how cricket, more than any sport, is forever appealing to its players to uphold values and respect traditions. As I reread that last sentence, I realise that I, too, have gone and done it. I have done what followers of the game often do when they are getting carried away with the its place in the grand scheme. I have referred to cricket as if it were a person, with needs, emotions and a sense of right and wrong.

Whisper it if you happen to be in the Lord's pavilion, but cricket is not a person. It is not a moral arbiter, a purveyor of ethics, a breeding ground for goodness. When Bishop Welldon of Calcutta told a Japanese audience in 1906 that 'There is no cricketer worthy of the name who would not be glad to sacrifice himself if he could so win the victory for his side,' the implication was that he had never watched W.G. Grace bat. Cricket is a sport, and a bloody good one. And if you watch sport in the hope that both sides will do their best to win, you have to accept that things happen in the heat of the moment. Yet those who have been lured into the trap of treating cricket as a way of life ascribe to it verbs that would make an opera diva blush. So it's hardly a surprise that cricket always seems to be wrestling with some crisis or other, many of them the result of impossibly high expectations in the first place. It's like grandpa getting ratty because you are not wearing a tie to breakfast.

In 2000, the MCC added a preamble to the Laws of cricket which captured the high-flown ideals the sport has burdened itself with. That's 'Laws', by the way. Not 'laws'. And certainly not 'rules'. Revelling in portentous upper case, it went like this: 'The Spirit of the Game involves respect for: Your opponents. Your own captain and team. The role of the umpires. The game's traditional values.' Now I'm all for respecting opponents, especially if they are bigger than me, and I have a strange aversion to anyone who might be tempted to take a lethal weapon to a match official. But the game's traditional values? What exactly are these and who determined them in the first place? Wasn't Jasper Vinall killed in 1624 by a flailing bat as he tried to catch the ball? Didn't Thomas 'Shock' White produce a bat as wide as the stumps at a match in Hambledon in 1771? And why else did Warwick Armstrong respond to Lord Harris's spluttered contention that 'people don't bet on cricket' by offering to place £500 'on the next Test, my Lord'? One man's set of traditional values has always been another's opportunity for a quick buck. Undeterred, the MCC preamble goes on to list a few of the crimes which are deemed to be against the Spirit of the Game. Among them are 'to appeal knowing that the batsman is not out' and 'to seek to distract an opponent either verbally or by harassment with persistent clapping or unnecessary noise under the guise of enthusiasm and motivation of one's own side'. In other words, the habits of all first-class cricketers, driven by honourable enough motives that range from playing for their country to ensuring a new contract, fall short of the game's exacting standards. And they do it every day of their playing lives.

If you think that's libellous, then consider the view of Rohan Kanhai, the West Indies batsman who kept wicket in place of the injured Clyde Walcott during the famous stand of 411 between Peter May and Colin Cowdrey against West Indies at Edgbaston in 1957. History views the partnership as the birth of pad-play, as May and Cowdrey destroyed the career of one of cricket's original mystery spinners, Sonny Ramadhin, by using their back leg as a last line of defence. Ramadhin bowled 98 overs in that innings – a Test record – and went up for as many shouts for leg-before. But according to Tony Francis's *The Zen of Cricket*, Kanhai believed that 'at least seven of the one hundred or so lbw appeals were out'. At least? Even bearing in mind the fact that Ramadhin probably wanted to do something nasty to May and Cowdrey with a stump, the implication that the other 93 appeals were *not* out hardly sits easily with the Game's Spirit. And if that doesn't convince you that the players and the administrators occasionally seem to come from different universes, try to imagine applying the same set of guidelines to football. 'Right, son, I'm booking you for making an unnecessary noise under the guise of enthusiasm. Clap like that once more and you're off!' Yet cricket, somehow, rarely falls off its high horse, even when it turns into a bucking bronco. It's enough to make you want to weep. Just make sure your tears don't earn you a ticking-off from the match referee for excessive show of emotion.

The notion that cricket began on a lofty pedestal only to embark on an endless, slippery slope has been around since time immemorial, which is when some lovers of the game would like you to believe it was conceived. Other writers – notably Derek Birley in *The Willow Wand* and Simon Rae in *It's Not Cricket* – have outlined the reasons behind cricket's self-positioning on the moral high ground, among them the rise of muscular Christianity in the English public-school system of the mid-19th century. By 1921, the good Lord Harris was waxing pompously about the widespread use of the phrase 'it's not cricket'. (As if it settled the matter, Harris was once described by his fellow establishment figure Pelham Warner as 'a trustee of the Marylebone Cricket Club, and a former captain of Eton, of Oxford, of Kent, of the Gentlemen, and of England'.) Now, without batting an eyelid, he declared this phrase, which these days is the most overused of all cricket's clichés, to be 'the brightest gem ever won by any pursuit: in constant use on the platform, in the pulpit, Parliament, and the press, to dub something as being not fair, not honourable, not noble. What a tribute for a game to have won . . . !'

But if being unfair, dishonourable and ignoble qualify as 'not cricket', then plenty of cricket in Lord Harris's days was, well, not cricket at all. Even Douglas Jardine, the man who cooked up Bodyline in his obsession to silence Bradman, lapsed into the realms of the wishy-washy by quoting a New Zealander who once described cricket as 'that beautiful, beautiful game which is battle and service and sport and art'. Delete 'battle', 'service' and 'art' and Jardine might have been on safer territory. Because in the real world cricket has often limboed below beauty. And to make the point, we don't even need to dip into the assorted crimes of W.G. Grace, who was once said to have shouted 'I declare' seconds before being caught.

Cricket's mythologians would have us believe that sledging is a modern phenomenon invented by the Australians to assert their *über*-virility over the sickly Poms and the rest. Considering that many of these mythologians are Englishmen, this view is hardly surprising. But what are we to make, for example, of an incident that took place at Canterbury, New Zealand, in 1903 involving none other than Bernard Bosanquet, the father of the googly? Bosanquet played his cricket for Eton, Oxford, Middlesex and England, so it's fair to say he might have come across the words of the poem by Sir Henry Newbolt, 'Vitaï Lampada'. Newbolt shamelessly transposed the 'breathless hush in the Close tonight' when there was 'ten to make and the match to win' into the field of military battle: 'The Gatling's jammed and the Colonel dead,/And the regiment blind with dust and smoke./The river of death has brimmed his banks,/And England's far, and Honour a name . . .'. He concluded that the most manly way to face certain death was to 'Play up! Play up! And play the game!' After all, if you had emerged unscathed from the life-threatening horrors of 'a bumping pitch and a blinding light', what possible reason was there to fear a bullet in the neck? More pertinently, why would you ever question the honour of the opposition when there is far more honour to be had in playing up and playing the game?

'Vitaï Lampada', the definitive hymn to cricket's self-regard, was written in 1897, which gave Bosanquet six years to consider its message before the ruckus at Canterbury. There, he was convinced he had bowled the home side's

No. 3 batsman, Walter Pearce, round his legs and was astonished to see him stay put. The umpire at the non-striker's end said his view had been obscured by Pearce's body, while the official at square-leg had been ducking in anticipation of a blow on the head. Turning to Arthur Sims, the other not-out batsman and a man who was later knighted for his services to commerce, Bosanquet is reported to have said: 'You're a nice cheat. I bowled him round his legs. Anybody could see that.' Now, while this is not exactly the same as receiving a shower of asterisked abuse from Andre Nel, it was pretty devastating repartee by the standards of the day. And – true to cricketing form – it sparked a disproportionate degree of outrage. The local paper was in little doubt: 'For English gentlemen to so far forget themselves as to openly dispute such a decision, and to say that it was the worst decision they had ever heard, was strange conduct,' it pontificated, pausing only to light a cigar and top up the gin.

Six years later, Jack Hobbs was batting for England against Australia at Headingley. Hobbs was a true gent, the kind of batsman who would give away his wicket after scoring one of his world-record 197 first-class centuries because it was unseemly to go on. (I tend to have the same predicament when I reach double figures.) But he had barely begun his international career when he set off for a run in the third Test, slipped and disturbed his wicket. Not out, said the umpire. The Australians had probably never read 'Vitaï Lampada' and might have found a particular use for it in a certain section of the dressing room if they had. Hobbs takes up the story in *My Cricket Memories*. 'The Australians made a rare fuss,' he whimpered. 'They gathered together on the field and confabulated. The chief offender was Warwick Armstrong, who got very nasty and unsportsmanlike, refusing to accept the umpire's decision. This upset me. I did not know whether I was standing on my head or my heels, with the consequence that two balls later I let one go, never even attempting to play it, and it bowled me.' Hobbs called it confabulation, which sounds like a crime only cricket could dream up. A century later Steve Waugh called it mental disintegration. These days it might be more colourful, and the insults might involve more family members than they did when Armstrong and his cohorts were at their confabulatory worst. But whatever you call it, sledging is not new.

In some ways we shouldn't be surprised by the prevalence in cricket of 'verbals', a classic piece of old pro's shorthand that covers anything from the witty to the downright offensive. Cricket is in theory a non-contact sport, which – for those wishing to unsettle – places the emphasis on words rather than sticks and stones. Imagine locking twenty-two drunks in a pub and telling them they had to win an argument without touching each other: the result would be all manner of violent wordplay. One-liners would take the place of a quick headbutt; a catalogue of insults would equate to fisticuffs. And while I'm not for one minute suggesting that cricketers regularly take the field still slurring their words from the pedalo trip the night before, the point is clear: a well-placed barb can be as lethal as a Richard Hadlee leg-cutter. Mike Brearley condemns sledging as 'a totally unwelcome aberration in the game, inane, humourless and unacceptable'. But that may have as much to do with his own decency as anything else. Inane? Often. Humourless? Sometimes, but not necessarily. (Who failed to laugh when Darren Gough decided to remind

Shane Watson of his skirmish with a ghost in Chester-le-Street's Lumley Castle by walking past him at the non-striker's end and shouting 'woooh!'?) Unacceptable? Depends on your point of view. But an aberration? Bosanquet, Armstrong and countless others suggest not.

Growing up, I always regarded sledging – which derives from the phrase 'subtle as a sledgehammer' and received a stamp of legitimacy under Ian Chappell's Australians in the 1970s – as one of those things that happened only rarely, such as Graeme Hick lasting more than twenty minutes against an obscenely angry Merv Hughes. (Hughes would later claim he took a quarter of his wickets by unsettling the batsman with a verbal lashing first.) 'Mervyn, Mervyn what has poor Mr Hick ever done to you?' asked an exasperated Dickie Bird as Hughes's sledging began to disturb birds in trees several miles away. 'He offended me in a former life,' came the surprisingly sharp-witted reply. Sure, cricket history was replete with stories of on-field witticisms, but most of them seemed too good to be true. Did Walter Hammond really mutter 'fine fucking way to start a series' after Don Bradman seemed to nick Bill Voce to Jack Ikin at slip on 28 in the first post-war Ashes Test? (Bradman, wouldn't you know it, went on to make 187 and Australia won by an innings and 332.) It would have been like telling the Queen to stuff it. And what self-respecting England fielder would have allowed his own team-mate to belittle him for letting the ball through his legs? 'Sorry, I should have kept them closed,' said the ingénu to Fred Trueman. 'Aye,' came Trueman's supposed reply. 'And so should your mother.'

And yet, sledging, it became apparent even before I had read about Bosanquet and Armstrong, was as common as muck, and often less clean. As the wise old Australian cricket journalist Ray Robinson wrote of Chappell's language: 'Players of their vintage have no aversion to biological verbs and nouns from Anglo-Saxon village vernacular long ostracised by refined society.' I once played for a team in which one of the bowlers was a woman, and the biology resided exclusively in the nouns. 'Whatever you do,' our wicketkeeper would say to the batsman as she approached the crease, 'don't look at her breasts.' The keeper claimed the tactic had a higher strike rate than any of his less mammary-related insults.

The harsh truth, however, is that most teams do not have the luxury of a bouncing bosom to take their wickets for them. West Indies would generally make do with long, languid stares of the kind you might get from the skinhead in the pub who suspects you're eyeing up his missus, or pint of Diamond White. 'He didn't say much,' said Steve Waugh of Curtly Ambrose, 'so you didn't know if he hated your guts. The West Indies side said nothing when I first started and you went out there intimidated. You just didn't know what was going to happen.' Ambrose's legendary reluctance to talk extended to journalists. One British tabloid reporter tried to get round the problem by asking Viv Richards, whom he knew, to put in an interview request with Curtly on his behalf. As the reporter waited outside the dressing-room door, Ambrose – 6 ft 7 in of insouciant indifference – appeared. 'You want to talk to Curtly?' he inquired. 'Yes, please.' 'You want to talk to Viv, you ask Viv. You want to talk to Curtly, you ask Curtly.' 'Fair enough. So, can I talk to Curtly then?' 'No. Curtly talks to no one.'

On the pitch, the worst West Indian sledging occurred when team-mates would tell Courtney Walsh to 'perform the operation', which might have put all kinds of unpleasant injuries and implements into the batsman's mind. But the West Indians had nothing on the Australians. That man Hughes, a creature Steve Waugh once nominated in a magazine Q&A as his 'favourite animal' and Shane Warne called 'basically a child in the body of an adult', earned this eulogy from Mike Atherton: 'He was all bristle and bullshit and I couldn't make out what he was saying, except that every sledge ended with "arsewipe".' Years later at a Test in Perth, I sat through a lunchtime speech from Hughes, now an Australian selector but still referred to at every third mention as a 'character', in which a suspicious number of anecdotes seemed to end with someone telling someone else to 'piss off'. Each punchline would bring the house down, as if the audience was having its memory bank wiped clean every few seconds. On the other side of the coin, Atherton wrote that he heard Hick sledge only once during his Test career, and that was when he came on as a substitute fielder against Sri Lanka. Atherton wondered whether Hick's uncharacteristic show of aggression was encouraged by the fact that he wouldn't have to bat. The psychology of sledging is worth a book in itself.

Mark Taylor, once Hughes's captain, declared – presumably while crossing his fingers behind his back – that 'I can't think of any player who has been put off his game by verbal abuse'. His what-me-sir? perspective was less than convincing. After all, Graham Thorpe has admitted that he was goaded into having a terminal thrash at Shane Warne by the garrulous Australian wicketkeeper Ian Healy during the 1993 Edgbaston Test. And many bitter England fans with long memories, of which there are a few, are convinced Warne talked Nasser Hussain into haring fatally down the pitch at a crucial stage of a one-day final at Sydney in 1999. Perhaps the two men's descriptions of the incident reflect the extent to which sledging on the field can at times be a mere precursor to sledging off it. Here's the Warne version: 'His face was red and you could almost see the steam coming out of his ears . . . It was one of the few occasions sledging worked . . . I could have been made to look like an idiot, but Nasser fell hook, line and sinker.' And here's Hussain: 'Please don't accuse me of losing the plot, allowing Shane Warne to get in my head and throwing it away in a huff . . . It really, honestly, wasn't the case at all.' Hussain himself later got into trouble after trying to stir things up during the Sri Lanka–England series in 2003–04 by allegedly greeting Muttiah Muralitharan's arrival at the crease with the words: 'Here he comes, the fucking cheat, the fucking chucker.' And the public interest in one of the game's supposed dark arts is such that Hussain's Essex colleague Ronnie Irani once had to issue a statement following a spat in a county game with Warne in which he denied that Warne had called his mother a 'whore'. 'I can categorically state,' stated Irani categorically, 'that Shane did not say anything inappropriate about my mother.'

The best sledges tend to be more subtle, even if they seem to involve female relatives a little too often for comfort (which is obviously the point: it would be a rubbish sledge that put a batsman at ease). The Australian wicket-keeper Tim Zoehrer once said to Phil Edmonds: 'At least I have an identity. You're just Frances Edmonds's husband.' Rod Marsh greeted Ian Botham with the query: 'How's your wife? And my kids?' Kevin Pietersen reacted to a barrage of short balls from the hapless Shane Watson during a one-dayer in Bristol by spanking him for four and running down the ground shouting 'Just because no one loves you any more', which was a reference to Watson's recent split with his girlfriend. Then there's Geoff Boycott and his commentary-box sledge which insists his mum could have done better with one of her sticks of rhubarb. A recent estimate placed her career average only fractionally behind Bradman's.

Robert Croft, who was once sledged himself by a national cricket correspondent by being termed 'a dumpy druid', took subtlety to new heights whenever Glamorgan played Gloucestershire and Jack Russell walked out to bat. Russell revelled in his eccentricity. He would never eat his beloved Weetabix unless they had been soaked in milk for a precise amount of time – historians believe the figure is somewhere between eight and twelve minutes. His diet on tour consisted of baked beans, and the same tea bag would be reused for days on end. When he applied his painting skills to self-portraiture, his young daughter observed: 'Dad, you've got madness in your eyes.' He liked that. But the detail Croft chose to home in on was the fact that Russell hated anyone knowing his address. Not even his team-mates knew where to send a Christmas card, and legend has it that builders working on his house had to be picked up at a pre-arranged venue before being driven blindfolded all the way to Russell's home. All it needed was for Croft to whisper 'we know where you live' and Russell would get twitchy. 'He didn't like it,' one of Croft's former Glamorgan team-mates told me.

And the lamest sledge? That prize, oddly enough, goes to Paul Nixon, who was picked for England's one-day side in the winter of 2006–07 on the basis that he kept spirits up behind the stumps (read: knew how to annoy the bejesus out of opposition batsmen). Yet when Steve James went out to bat in a county match for Glamorgan against Leicestershire, all Nixon could come up with was 'Let's get county cricket's gentleman out.' James was so stunned by this slap across the back of the hand with a piece of wet lettuce that his reply was an incredulous 'What?' Nixon's explanation took the chat even further down the path of the Women's Institute: 'Couldn't think of anything else. I haven't got anything on you.'

The tactic need not be exclusively aimed at batsmen, though. During England's traumatic tour of Australia in 1974–75, Tony Greig decided to take on Dennis Lillee by providing running commentary for free on his own innings. 'That's four, take that!' Greig would say after slapping Lillee through the covers. And when he hit the next ball for four as well, he went down on one knee to signal the boundary, as I had been tempted to do in the Lord's nets against Andrew Flintoff. 'There you go, four more.' Batting at the other end, Dennis Amiss recalled thinking: 'Lillee was absolutely seething. I knew we were in for a hell of a tour.' England lost 4–1. Steve Waugh would rouse himself by instigating a verbal battle with the fielders. England noticed this and decided to give him the silent treatment as he walked out to bat at Old Trafford in 1997. According to England's captain Mike Atherton, Waugh worked out pretty quickly what was going on. 'OK, you're not talking to me, are you?' he said, as if stunned that England weren't calling him a convict. 'Well, I'll talk to myself then.' As Atherton put it in his autobiography: 'And he did, for 240 minutes in the first innings, and 382 minutes in the second.' England were damned if they sledged and doubly damned if they didn't, although fairness demands the telling of another Waugh story in which his renowned mental fortitude was made to look slightly foolish. Walking out to bat in a Test against New Zealand, he told the fielders who were still busy celebrating the fall of the last wicket: 'You won't be laughing so bloody hard when I'm still here in six hours' time.' He was out next ball.

But the most bizarre example of on-field chat surely comes from Carlisle Best, the West Indian batsman who saved his best lines for, er, himself. Australia's David Boon, who many believe grew a walrus moustache specifically so that his sub-helmet chunterings at short-leg would die a muffled death before they reached the umpires, recalled a typical example of Best's self-banter, which more often than not amounted to a gratuitously solipsistic piece of commentary. 'And Best faces up to Alderman, who's at the top of his mark. He's one of the world's best swing bowlers. He comes in with his fluent and powerful run-up, he lets it go . . . and Best lets it pass outside off-stump. You should have hit that for four, Carlisle Best!' Even when Best did make a comment aimed at the bowler, he was only ever really talking to himself. 'And Best rocks back and pulls it for four!' he would exclaim. 'Craig McDermott must surely know by now, you can't be bowling there to Carlisle Best.' It is perhaps no coincidence that Best's great nephew, Tino, who during the West Indian tour of England in 2004 took to sledging like a duck to one of his team's scorecards, was susceptible to a few well-chosen words in his ear. 'Mind the windows Tino,' cautioned Andrew Flintoff from slip as West Indies fought to save the first Test at Lord's. Moments later Best was stumped aiming to hit Ashley Giles into Regent's Park, and Flintoff was in stitches.

The fact is that sledging is either attacked or defended depending on the circumstances. Kumar Sangakkara, the Sri Lanka wicketkeeper who has trained as a lawyer, is particularly adept at applying his razor-sharp mind to making the batsman feel at home. When Nasser Hussain celebrated a long-overdue hundred at Kandy in 2001 with scary vigour, Sangakkara wrily noted: 'It's only a hundred. You haven't broken Lara's record.' Three years later, on the day after Muralitharan had reported Hussain to the authorities for calling him names, Sangakkara allegedly carried on as if nothing had happened. 'He was in my ear all the time,' remembered Hussain. 'About me losing the captaincy, that I was one innings away from retirement, that I had dropped Graeme Smith and he had gone on to a double hundred.' So there was general tittering at the back when Sangakkara insisted a couple of years later, apparently with a straight face, that sledging had no place in the game. Graeme Smith, the South Africa captain reprieved by Hussain, invited ridicule when he attempted to sledge the touring Australians during press conferences, and did not look much cleverer when Australia won the series at a canter. Yet Smith's coach, Mickey Arthur, was moved to describe Smith's tactics as 'very, very noble'. They were, he said, an attempt to divert the flak from his team-mates, which was certainly one way of looking at it. At the less noble end of the spectrum, Allan Border responded to Robin Smith's request for a mid-innings glass of water by spitting: 'What do you think this is? A fucking tea party? No you can't have a fucking glass of water. You can fucking wait like all the rest of us.' The truth is that such charming byplay is not to everyone's taste. Subjective judgements play more of a role than most people are willing to admit.

The same goes for the game's other grey areas. Take walking, a harmless enough activity outside cricket, but a hotbed of ethical intrigue within it. Old-school decorum requires a batsman to give himself out if he knows he has nicked the ball. Yet, with one or two exceptions, no professional batsman in his right mind has given himself out since about 1961. And even before that there was a suspicion that known walkers would pick and choose their moments so that they could con the umpire the next time they edged it on 99. I have always been an instinctive walker, not because I'm more ethical than the next man, but because I look so guilty when I know I am out that there seems little point staying put. The habit is so ingrained that I once gave myself lbw seconds before the umpire did the deed for me. 'Never seen that before,' muttered Simon Hughes, the next man in, as we crossed in the outfield. I half-expected to see the moment analysed on national TV shortly afterwards. 'Now, several of you have emailed in to ask what constitutes naivety on the cricket field . . .'

Derek Birley argues that walking became popular among amateur batsmen keen to show their superiority over the umpires, whom they regarded as card-carrying members of the lumpen proletariat. And that, the argument goes, explains why the custom never caught on among the far less hierarchical Australians. Adam Gilchrist staged a one-man attempt to alter the perception that the only time an Australian walks is when the truck has run out of petrol. Yet his famous decision to give himself out in the semi-final of the 2003 World Cup against Sri Lanka was, according to Gilchrist's autobiography, met with stony silence in the dressing room, which serves him right for calling the book *Walking to Victory*. 'Already I feel somewhat alienated from my team-mates,' he wrote, as if he expected them to bear him shoulder-high along Port Elizabeth's seafront. 'They don't have to say anything more. Of course they're pissed off with my sudden decision to form a closer relationship with my conscience. I wish someone would say something so that I could blab out some poor, nervous excuse, but no one does. We watch the rest of the innings in silence.' Gilchrist calls it 'one of those split-second decisions that can change the course of a game, or even a life. But even during this lonely stroll against the grain, somewhere deep in the back of my mind, something is reminding me: you're doing the right thing.'

Others felt he became slightly evangelical, and were amused to see Gilchrist wrongly giving himself out caught at slip against Bangladesh two years later after the ball had flown at a strange angle out of a foot-hole. A few struggled to square his new-found tendency to walk with some of his more fanciful appeals from behind the stumps. Some wondered whether he would walk at a crucial moment of an Ashes decider. Several applauded his honesty and wished all batsmen would follow suit. But if the mixed reaction to Gilchrist's attitude showed anything, it was that the so-called ethics of cricket, supposedly a universal concept, inspires anything but a consensus.

How desirable is walking, in any case? And doesn't it say everything about cricket's navel-gazing that we are discussing it in the first place? After all, you don't expect a footballer to hold his hands up after a theatrical dive and implore the referee not to book his opponent. Or a prop forward to emerge from the bottom of a ruck and hare after the referee to point out that he has just gouged his opposite number's left eye. So why on earth should a Test batsman, his career perhaps on the line, be expected to be complicit in his own downfall? There have been plenty of cases in which the umpire has been made to look pretty stupid when players, however well-intentioned, have taken the Laws into their own hands. In one instance, the New Zealand captain Walter Hadlee, father of Richard, even insisted on Cyril Washbrook continuing with his innings during a Test match because Hadlee disagreed with the umpire's decision to uphold a shout for lbw. In another, more surreal, example, the Australian all-rounder George 'Harry' Trott, surrendered his wicket to England's Johnny Briggs the ball after the umpire had failed to grant a convincing appeal for a stumping. 'Little Briggsy had bowled himself inside out trying to trap me,' explained Trott. 'Why should he be robbed because [umpire] West was out late last night?' Imagine Ricky Ponting surrendering his wicket like that to Monty Panesar because 'Monty morally got me the ball before, mate'. Nah, me neither.

If most modern cricketers are agreed that walking is an unrealistic business, then the arcane practice of ball-tampering causes even more divisions. And it wasn't until I was covering a county championship match between Surrey and Nottinghamshire at The Oval in 2005 that the exact nature of these divisions struck me. Crudely put, the two groups most likely to throw their hands up in horror at the crime of lifting the seam are journalists who never played the game to any great level and batsmen who have just been blown away by a series of unplayable yorkers. The group most likely to tell the non-ex-playing hacks and the batsmen to get a life and catch some real criminals instead are hard-bitten ex-pros in the press box and bowlers, who spend most of their time grumbling that cricket is a batsman's game anyway. Idealism on one side, realism on the other. That day at The Oval, reaction to Surrey's breach of Law 42.3 – cricket's Laws, like its batting and bowling averages, go in for decimal points – revealed a lot about the game's two faces: the public show of outrage and the private shrug of the shoulders. The reporters at the ground – including this one – criticised Surrey for the lame statement they issued the day after they had twice been caught lifting the ball's quarter-seam, only for the ex-pros in the broadsheets to point out that ball-tampering was a harsh fact of life, and you'd better get used to it, sonny. After that you could barely open your front door without bumping into a retired seam bowler with a story to tell about the time he chewed chunks out of the ball moments before taking five for three at Swansea in 1974. Ex-pros began reminiscing with rheumy eyes – which they still managed to wink conspiratorially – about team-mates who had been designated official 'ball-polishers'. I hadn't intended to be sanctimonious in my reporting of the story, but I suddenly felt as out of touch as the former president of the MCC who once marched into the press box at Hove to tell the assembled hacks that he had an 'announcement' to make. It turned out that on the previous day he had walked onto the pitch during a schoolboy match to instruct the players to stop their infernal clapping and squawking. We quietly thanked him for the exclusive.

But it was the openness of some ex-players which really hit home. We had all heard the stories about Imran Khan taking to the field for Sussex armed with a bottle opener and a glint in his eye, but lazy western prejudices could comfortably put that down to the nodding acquaintance between Pakistan's cricketers and the Laws. One England batsman I spoke to after the Oval Test in 2006 had been forfeited by Pakistan following Darrell Hair's accusation of changing the condition of the ball was in sarcastic mood. 'You can't accuse Pakistan of ball-tampering,' he told me on condition of anonymity. 'You just can't do it. It creates an international incident. The righteous indignation does make me laugh. We all know where the tampering came from, and who is best at it. Now they're saying there's no evidence. It all sounds a bit convenient for me.' Yet was he in any position to mount the high horse? Was anyone? Two days after that Test was cancelled, I spoke to the Pakistan coach, the late Bob Woolmer, who cheerfully admitted that lifting the seam to create unpredictable movement off the pitch was quite simply the done thing. 'Every single bowler I know from the time I played, between 1968 and 1984, was guilty of some sort of – under the current law – ball-changing,' he said, as casually as if he had just asked me to pass the salt and pepper. 'I remember getting the ball in 1969 as a rookie [for Kent against Sussex at Canterbury] and the seam was razor sharp. I nearly cut my nails on it. I was about to take it to the umpires, but I was pulled away and told just to get on and bowl. And I remember going on to take 7 for 47. I never touched it, but every time it came back from the other end it was like a razor.'

Woolmer went on to explain that there was more than one way to skin a batsman. 'Eventually they taught me other tricks. When I went to South Africa, they weren't allowed to use sweat from the forehead to apply to the ball. They were only allowed to use sweat from under the armpits. So I was given two tubes of lip-ice. I rubbed it into my hands and then into my armpits. It was like glue. If you haven't played the game, like a lot of the umpires haven't, they don't know these things. The more laws you make to try to stop it being done, the more the players go the other way – like prohibition. The more you stop alcohol, the more you go underground. They really need to open it up in my opinion.' He advocated scrapping the law which governs the condition of the ball, and imagined a utopian world – or possibly dystopian for the batsmen – where bowlers could do anything to it so long as they did not bring any implements with them onto the field. It was tricky trying to argue against ball-tampering after that.

Which brings us to the other illegal thing you can do with the ball. Chucking is a peculiarly cricketing type of crime because it offends against one of the game's funda-mental aesthetics: the straight arm. Cricket lovers like to think that the straight arm is what separates the sport from baseball, in the same way that Homo sapiens rejoices in the superiority of the opposable thumb. Yes, the straight arm is nothing less than proof that cricket is two rungs up the evolutionary ladder from its trans-Atlantic cousin, which is partly why Don Bradman, as ruthless an administrator as he was a batsman, weeded out the numerous chuckers in the Australian team in the late 1950s and early '60s. Bradman, under pressure from the MCC, wanted them out of the game, but not before they had thrown England to a 4–0 defeat in Australia in 1958–59 – revenge, as some saw it, for the deliberate doctoring of the pitches at Old Trafford (Jim Laker 19 for 90) and Headingley on Australia's previous visit to England in 1956. Peter May, the England captain on that harrowing tour, remembered watching one of the chuckers, Ian Meckiff, warming up ahead of the match against Victoria. 'One of them was throwing a ball at a batsman,' said May. 'This seemed an odd way for a bowler to limber up. A few minutes later he was out in the middle bowling to Peter Richardson with exactly the same action. I was fascinated.' Ah, that great English understatement.

But despite Bradman's best efforts, the problem raises its ugly elbow time and again, never more controversially than in the case of Muttiah Muralitharan, the Sri Lanka off-spinner who was humiliatingly no-balled seven times by the square-leg umpire Darrell Hair during a Test at Melbourne. Now, for what it's worth, and it isn't worth a lot, I don't believe Murali is a chucker. A genius with a deformed elbow and a wrist that is more flexible than a teenage Russian gymnast, yes. But a chucker, no. He once bowled with his right arm in a cast on Channel 4 to prove his point and still made the ball do loop-the-loops and sing for its supper. I have also seen slow-motion replays from the forearm down only – replays, in other words, that removed from sight his rubbery wrist. They did not look half as incriminating as replays that included the wrist, which suggests that the naked eye might be unduly influenced by the unusual goings-on of the less relevant joint. In defence of his critics, I have watched from the bird's-eye view of the Lord's media centre as Murali has bowled from the pavilion end and cringed at what appeared to be a blatant transgression of Law 24, which was altered in 2005 to allow the bowling arm to straighten by up to 15 degrees – the point at which, according to the ICC, a chuck becomes visible to the naked eye. But then optical illusion is so much part of Murali's skill as a bowler that it might almost be considered a part of his repertoire. Imagine Charles Colville screaming: 'Oh, he's only gone and done Andrew Strauss with the optical illusion, which at first sight seemed to have pitched outside off-stump and broken back to hit leg, whereas in actual fact replays show it simply went straight on between bat and pad!'

More than any other issue, chucking seems to bring out the lowest common denominator in us all. Murali's detractors – mainly white, even if the former Indian slow left-armer Bishan Bedi has labelled him a 'javelin thrower' – say that the ICC introduced the 15-degree threshold to circumvent the problem of Murali's doosra, where the kink had previously been measured as high as 14 degrees. One of them, Martin Crowe, even suggested that a bend of one degree should be illegal, in which case every single cricket match ever would have to be called off before it had even begun. Murali's supporters – mainly Asian – have pointed to an Anglo-Australian conspiracy which was hell-bent, as it were, on preventing the Sri Lankan from ever overtaking Shane Warne's Test record of 708 wickets.

And yet I have never thought of the chucking issue as a racial one. No Englishman will ever deny that the left-arm spinner Tony Lock used to throw his faster ball in the 1950s. The joke was – and how Lock must have laughed – that any batsman bowled by one of his quicker deliveries would complain he had been run out. The former Australia captain Lindsay Hassett went even further by shouting 'Strike one, strike two.' An exchange on the balcony at The Oval after England had somehow scraped a 1–0 series win in 1953 left little doubt either. 'England deserved to win, if not from the first ball at least from the second-last over,' Hassett said live on air. 'Well done, Lindsay, that was absolutely perfect,' said the former England captain Walter Robins, standing nearby. Hassett replied: 'Not bad, considering that Tony Lock chucked half our side out.' According to Ray Robinson's account: 'In the privacy of the Australian room a wall clock was pelted to ruins with actions no umpire would have passed.' More recently, the Pakistan Cricket Board set up a special scheme to help fifty-five bowlers in their own domestic game found to have a suspect action.

But the incident which settled the racist/non-racist argument for me took place during the New Zealand–India series in 2002–03. Several New Zealanders in Sky's commentary box were getting their 'knuckers' in a 'twust' about the action of the Kiwi opening bowler Kyle Mills. One of them was apparently threatening to voice his allegations live on air, but in the end settled for a back-of-the-box sideswipe after Mills was dismissed during one of the interminable one-day internationals. 'Fuck off, chucker' came the line, which rather detracted from the wit of Nasser Hussain's jibe at Murali a year later. When New Zealanders start abusing other New Zealanders – the Kiwis tend to take enormous pride in the achievements of their compatriots – you know racism has got nothing to do with it. Still, the game's ability to work up a head of steam about a degree here and two degrees there remains world-class, as if breaking the Laws is a worse crime in cricket than it is in any other sport.

And yet, in the first decade of the 21st century, we still find some funny things to get worked up about. In the aftermath of the 2005 Ashes, when most of us were drooling like proud grandparents over the sportsmanship shown by both sides, expectations changed once more, to the extent that the ICC felt they needed to issue a stern ticking-off when Australia and South Africa engaged in a tit-for-tat, testosterone-fuelled exchange of views ahead of their two series the following winter. No matter that Zimbabwean cricket was knee-deep in crisis. No, what was important was that one bronzed southern-hemisphere Adonis was blowing raspberries at another. And even calling him names! 'There have been a series of comments by players and former players ahead of the Australia v South Africa series that I believe make it necessary to remind the players of the importance of playing within the spirit of the game ahead of this series,' intoned a grave-sounding Malcolm Speed, the chief executive of the ICC. And with that warning in place, the world breathed again – at least until the Australians and Indians started being nasty to each other down under.

Personally, I preferred a joke cracked by Andrew Flintoff, who less than two years before he drunkenly fell off a pedalo in St Lucia was being feted as the Angel Gabriel himself for commiserating with Brett Lee while his team-mates celebrated England's two-run win in the Edgbaston Test against Australia. Asked at a staged Q&A session after the series had finished exactly what he had said to Lee as he put his arm round him and congratulated him for his efforts in getting so close, Flintoff replied: 'That's 1–1, you Aussie bastard.' Even the Spirit of the Game would have enjoyed that one.

6

THE UMPIRES

'NOBODY CAN now doubt that umpires have to endure terrific pressures in the blaze of modern publicity, that some players trade on that fact, and that the tendency must be stamped out. Any top-class umpire expects during his career to handle controversial incidents; now these rank as national disputes. The eyes and ears of the world are riveted on every Test match.'

Yes, for every good-natured Andrew Flintoff, putting his arm around a vanquished opponent, there is an anti-Flintoff, pushing the umpire to the brink of violence by shouting loud enough and often enough and hoping that, sooner or later, he will raise the 'fickle finger of fate' – as one young radio broadcaster described it live on-air to cruel titters in the Blackpool press tent. Opponents call this approach cheating; team-mates call it aggression; neutrals call it tedious. And the tendency is to regard it as a very recent phenomenon, as much a sign of the times as chavs, hoodies and Russell Brand. Yet the words of doom quoted in the first paragraph were penned in 1973 by the former Test umpire Frank Lee in the aftermath of the Arthur Fagg controversy at Edgbaston. Umpiring in his fourteenth Test, Fagg had become so incensed with what he regarded as the disrespect shown to him by the West Indian captain, Rohan Kanhai, that he had to be talked into carrying on with the game by his colleague, Dickie Bird, a man for whom controversy never seemed to involve more than a burst drain or a carefully hidden mobile phone. Thirty-five years on, Lee's brooding observations seem as apposite as ever.

The cricket world shudders like a pneumonic octogenarian when disrespect is shown to an umpire. For one thing, it seems to relegate the sport to the level of football, where players are applauded if they manage ninety minutes without pinning the referee in a headlock. But it also goes against one of cricket's holiest commandments, the one which would have been the first to be engraved on the stone tablet if it had been Dickie, not Moses, shuffling down Mount Sinai, doubtless grumbling about the light. The commandment? The Umpire's Decision Is Final. (Even if it is wrong, which – humans being humans – it occasionally is.) Now this is a very noble precept and it has the tendency to make cricket feel very pleased with itself. You could argue, for example, that this basic rule – drilled into youngsters along with the importance of always allowing your opponent first crack at the teatime plate of Victoria sponge – is what prevents the cricket equivalent of the former Sheffield Wednesday striker Paolo Di Canio's comedy shove on referee Paul Alcock. 'The umpires shall be the sole judges of fair and unfair play,' intones Law 3.7, the po-faced patriarch of cricket's dos and don'ts. And who could argue with that? Indeed, it all ties in with the standard metaphorical reading of cricket, one I have often used to wind up my cricket-indifferent friends, in which the umpire (God) dispenses judgement that is accepted unquestioningly by the batsman (mankind), who is then sent to the pavilion (heaven – or possibly hell, if he is out for a duck) to pack up his kit (get on with the afterlife). And in the case of one or two Australian umpires in the last fifteen years, the idea that the good Lord himself really is standing twenty-five yards away does not seem so ridiculous.

But there are a few problems with placing so much emphasis on this notion of finality. First, cricketers as a breed tend to be gentler creatures than footballers and hardly need reining in. This is partly because there are five days in which to get everything done, and screaming and shouting is not going to help anyone. It is also because, like most rugby players, they are generally bright enough to know that upsetting the man who holds your fate in his hands – to get all theological again – is not a career-enhancing move. To rejoice in the relatively good behaviour of cricketers is like telling a roomful of non-smokers they are not allowed to light up and then patting everyone on the back for their abstinence.

Second, not every umpire has stuck rigidly to the idea that their word is final. The legendary Frank Chester, who played for Worcestershire but turned to umpiring at the age of 26 after losing his right arm in the First World War, had a misleadingly definitive answer to a critic who wondered why he hadn't shown a batsman the benefit of the doubt. 'Doubt? When I'm umpiring there's never any doubt.' But Chester operated in a pre-television age, where any decision could be explained away with a quiet 'That pitched a fraction outside leg' or 'He nicked that', safe in the knowledge that Bob Willis could not take him apart in the Sky studio with the aid of Hawk-Eye, super slo-mos and Charles Colvile. What, you wonder, would Chester have made of Dave Orchard's decision to cave in to pressure from Hansie Cronje and refer the run-out of Graham Thorpe to the third umpire at Cape Town in January 1996? Orchard had initially ruled not out after Andrew Hudson had hit the stumps from backward square-leg, but when TV sets in the corporate boxes broadcast damning replays,

Cronje was alerted to the truth and – against the playing regulations – asked Orchard to refer his decision. Orchard obliged, and Thorpe was waved off Newlands by hundreds of inebriated Afrikaners. It was, said *Wisden*, 'perilously close to mob rule'. Cronje was fined half his match fee while Orchard admitted he had forgotten he was able to consult a replay.

And yet justice was done. Had the umpire's word been final, Thorpe might have played a substantial innings; England, not South Africa, might have won the five-Test rubber 1–0; and we might never have heard the full extent of the breakdown in relations between Ray Illingworth and Devon Malcolm – one of the most intriguing accounts of management–player relations there has ever been. Even Dickie Bird, a man of such thoroughness that he turned up for his first match as an umpire five hours early and was spotted by a policeman trying to scale the Oval gates, has exposed the question of finality as, well, a little too final. He once gave Kent's Graham Cowdrey out caught behind off Curtly Ambrose, only to recall Cowdrey when he was halfway back to the Canterbury pavilion because he decided the ball had actually brushed his forearm. Anyone who has seen Ambrose look thoroughly hacked off even when doing something he enjoys, like playing bass guitar for Big Bad Dread and the Baldhead or bowling beamers at Dermot Reeve, will understand the bravery of Bird's decision.

Third, a playing regulation was introduced into the 2007 Friends Provident Trophy which by definition undermined any rigid notion of finality. Based on an idea first mooted by Duncan Fletcher, each side in televised matches – where the technology was available – were allowed to refer at least two decisions to the third umpire, with a life lost for each incorrect challenge. So when Jeremy Lloyds gave the Sussex captain Chris Adams out lbw to the Somerset medium-pacer Peter Trego at Taunton on 29 April, a peeved Adams took a couple of steps towards the pavilion before deciding to appeal against the decision. Unfortunately for him – and 'to widespread surprise', according to one national newspaper report – the third umpire Barrie Leadbeater upheld the decision, presumably reasoning that he could only reverse Lloyds's call if it was 'beyond reasonable doubt' that he had made a 'clear and obvious mistake'. The ICC themselves had already toyed with the idea of introducing the concept for the little-loved Champions Trophy in India in 2006, but eventually decided against it, perhaps after studying several slow-motion replays of the committee meeting which first voted for the move. In the case of county cricket, the experiment did not work because third umpires were reluctant to overrule their mates on national TV. And it was not until the series between Sri Lanka and India in 2008 that the ICC felt brave enough to trial it at international level.

The differing reactions to the ICC committee's initial proposal was telling. In a for-and-against debate in the *Guardian*, the ubiquitous Dickie Bird came out fighting from the traditionalist corner. 'It is coming to the point, and I can see it arriving soon, when you will ask why the umpires are out in the middle at all,' he wailed. 'All they will do is count whether six balls have been bowled in an over and before long there will be something to do that for them too. Umpires will just turn into robots; it's sad for the game.' Why it should be 'sad' that the already high number of correct decisions made in cricket should increase even further was not explained, although Bird took refuge in the usual vocabulary of the misty-eyed. 'The central role of the umpire has been essential to the game's fabric throughout its history,' he said, 'and not allowing them to make decisions is a loss to cricket.' In the other corner was Bob Woolmer, who so loved technology that he was once reprimanded for wiring himself up to Hansie Cronje, the captain of the South African team he coached, at the 1999 World Cup to impart snippets of tactical advice. The referrals experiment, he argued, would be 'merely another opportunity to make the game as fair as possible'. But more of this later.

It is pretty obvious, then, that the umpire's word is final, unless he changes his mind, at which point it finally becomes final; or unless a player challenges him under the new proposals, in which case he can be made to look very foolish by his mate in the third umpire's box; or unless the umpire happens to do what Peter Hartley did on his debut as an international umpire in 2007 and decide that his decision not to refer the run-out of Paul Collingwood was wrong after glancing up at the replay shown on the big screen; or unless a batsman's team-mates have seen the replays and are now waving frantically at him from the dressing-room balcony to stay put, as per Kevin Pietersen in a Lord's Test against India. Apart from all those instances, the umpire's word is final.

In some cases, the finality seems strangely inevitable. Mike Brearley recalls being wrongly given out on a tour of India by an umpire who later apologised to him for his error. 'I'm sorry, Mr Brearley,' he said. 'I knew it wasn't out but my hand started moving upwards and I couldn't do anything to stop it.' And the former New Zealand official Steve Dunne occasionally provided a heart-stopping twist to the myth of finality by beginning to raise his finger only to think better of it halfway through. The look on England fast bowler Chris Lewis's face in 1992 when he realised Dunne's raised digit was now heading in the other direction could be the closest a bowler has come to coitus interruptus in full view of the cameras.

A change of mind, however, is the least of it. Whisper it, but the notion that cricketers have always looked to the umpire for the last word on objectivity is a fanciful one too. During Australia's tour of England in 1899, the tourists were slightly put out to see umpire Dick Barlow, a former Lancashire opener who was so dogged that he once carried his bat for an innings of five, celebrating the run-out of Clem Hill in the Trent Bridge Test before the fielders had actually appealed. And even before that, when cricket existed to keep the bookies happy and massage the egos of a few pompous grandees, no umpire would have lasted long in the job if he had based his decisions on anything as controversial as what actually happened out on the pitch. Simon Rae points out that the earliest set of surviving cricket rules, dating back to 1727 and the matches between sides owned by the Duke of Richmond and Mr Alan Broderick, heir to Viscount Middleton, stated: 'If any of the gamesters shall speak or give their opinion on any point of the game, they are to be turned out, and voided in the match.' This reasonable stipulation, however, came with a caveat: it was 'not to extend to the Duke of Richmond and Mr Broderick', who would 'on their honours' deal with any 'doubt or dispute'. If umpires today grumble that they are being reduced to hatstands by the inevitable creep of technology, at least they do not have to worry that their career might come to a mysteriously swift conclusion if they trigger the local landowner.

Yet this freedom to give anyone out at any stage of the game without fearing a visit from a pair of Phil Mitchell lookalikes is only a recent development. Frank Chester was standing in his first county game at Leyton, between Essex and Somerset, when he gave decisions against both captains, Johnny Douglas and John Daniell. His colleague at the other end warned him that he would be 'signing his death warrant' if he continued like that, which seemed an interesting take on the concept of impartiality. Captains fill out reports at the end of every match and umpires are among the many issues they must assess. Saw off the skipper, and your mark out of ten might be lucky to reach single figures. Later in his career, as if to prove the point, Douglas reckoned the loss of the Essex captaincy cost him around 30 wickets and 200 runs a season, which must have been a depressing realisation – like your girlfriend telling all and sundry you're a demon in the sack before ending things the moment you lose that high-flying job in the City.

Now, I am not for a moment suggesting that the vast majority of umpires are not dedicated, honest men who make tremendous sacrifices to oversee a game they love. The county circuit is full of them. David Constant and Alan Whitehead used to travel the country in caravans to save some of their puny allowances, while Roy Palmer could only travel around the country at the speed of a slow off-break after converting a single-decker bus into his very own mobile abode. To do the job professionally is to embark on a labour of love, and an often unrequited one at that. In the itinerant world of the international game, no one is lonelier than the umpires and match official: Mike Procter, one of the ICC's match referees, reckons he spends an average of 170 nights away from home a year.

But when one group of competitive men are trying to persuade a figure of supposedly unimpeachable objectivity to spoil the day for another group of competitive men, tempers will flare, mistakes will be made and accusations hurled. In the days before the ICC agreed to introduce two neutral umpires – Dickie Bird prefers 'independent', since neutrality implies that what went before was anything but – it was common practice to accuse the country you had just toured (and probably lost in) of possessing the worst officials ever known to man. 'In Britain we have the finest in the world because they are practically full-time professionals,' blustered Fred Trueman in *Ball of Fire*, published in 1977. 'In Australia I found they could go either way, in India they were terrible – I remember once in Bombay on an exhibition tour putting a man out four times before he actually went back to the pavilion – but in the West Indies they have the worst in the world.' And that was the edited version.

The white cricket nations have generally patted themselves on the back à la Trueman and gained strength from each other's denigration of the rest of the world's umpires. In some cases, the criticism has been justified. The growth of YouTube has presented us with gems that would otherwise remain hidden, such as the Pakistani umpire Shakeel Khan giving Mike Gatting out lbw to Abdul Qadir at Lahore in 1987–88 almost before the bowler had appealed. The sight of Gatting, who had missed a sweep shot, down on one knee, his head slumped on his bat handle in disbelief, seemed to encapsulate English frustration with the subcontinent. But these are easy and unhelpful stereotypes. And for every decision not given against Javed Miandad – it took him nine years to be given out lbw in a home Test, by which time he had amassed over 3,000 runs in Pakistan at an average of 81 – there are plenty of tales that do not reflect well on the supposedly more fair-minded officials of the older cricketing nations.

Think, for example, of England's visit to Australia in 1970–71. In those days, before the Law changed to the one we know and love today, the regulations down under stated that the ball had to pitch on the stumps before the umpire could think about upholding an lbw appeal. Inevitably, leg before was a much less common dismissal than it is today. And that in part explains why Australia only managed to wring five decisions out of their own umpires all series. But England did not win a single lbw appeal in six Tests. 'You'd have thought one or two of them might have been out,' Ray Illingworth, the England captain on that trip, told me several decades later. Had England not won 2–0 to regain the Ashes for the first time in fifteen years, that statistic would have been aired a lot more times than it has been. I asked the Anglo-Australian cricket historian David Frith what he remembered about England's frustrations. 'Their problem was that the Australian umpires seemed to have come to some sort of agreement that the sweep shot as executed against Illingworth by batsmen such as Peter Burge could not reasonably be given out lbw when they missed the ball,' he replied. 'It was very, very frustrating, and had Hawk-Eye been in existence then, a change of attitude might have been forced upon Lou Rowan, Tom Brooks and Max O'Connell (though Rowan in particular was extremely stubborn). I recall that as the series wore on, it was apparent that the Australians knew that the sweep was a safe shot whatever the path of the ball, and it was used to profusion.' Illingworth was not the only England bowler tearing his hair out. Indeed, that series is generally remembered for the views of the England fast bowler John Snow on Mr Rowan: 'I have never come across another umpire so stubborn, lacking in humour, unreasonable and utterly unable to distinguish between a delivery short of a length and a genuine bouncer which goes through head high.' Apart from that, Snow and Rowan were practically joined at the hip.

In fact, there is a school of – mainly non-Australian – thought which says Australian umpires got away with it for far too long. Sunil Gavaskar certainly thought so after he was given out lbw to Dennis Lillee at Melbourne in February 1981 by Rex Whitehead, who was standing in his first series. Club players will be familiar with the arm-waving batsman, pointing to his bat to indicate an inside edge and looking around for sympathy from fielders who would be the first to complain if it happened to them but start spitting feathers if the dissent stems from the opposition. But Gavaskar did more than wave his arms. He grabbed his bemused opening partner Chetan Chauhan – famous mainly for this incident and the fact that he managed to score over 2,000 Test runs without ever making a century – and would have successfully persuaded him to leave the field of play in protest had the Indian management not intervened on the boundary. 'I was infuriated by the injustice of it all,' Gavaskar explained, perhaps believing he was the first player in the history of the game who wanted to wrap his willow around an umpire's head. 'Whitehead has stood in all three Tests, and many bad decisions by him have gone against us.' Lillee's take on the matter was less conspiratorial. 'He spat the dummy right out of the pram.' Make up your own mind with the help of YouTube.

Phil Tufnell recalls an incident during the Boxing Day Test at Melbourne in 1990, a game which England lost after their last six second-innings wickets fell for three runs against the beanpole left-armer Bruce Reid, who always reminded me of the nightmarishly gangly tailor who cuts off the thumbs of a little boy in Heinrich Hoffmann's *Struwwelpeter*. Tufnell's version of events is that he asked the Australian umpire Peter McConnell how many balls were left in the over and was met with the following reply: 'Count 'em yourself, you Pommie c**t.' The best bit about the story is Tufnell's surprise when his captain, Graham Gooch – with whom relations had not been at their most cordial – walked over to defend him. 'I heard what you said and you cannot talk to my players like that,' said Gooch to McConnell. Tufnell's reaction? 'You could have tied my tits together with candyfloss.' (Gooch, after all, would later joke that the best thing about Tufnell's bowling was that he wasn't fielding.) Later in the innings, Tufnell was convinced he had David Boon caught behind, only for McConnell to look 'me straight in the eye' and say 'not out'. 'You fucking bastard,' said Tufnell, buttering up the umpire in time-honoured tradition. 'Now *you* can't talk to *me* like that, Phil,' said McConnell. He might not have been on Tufnell's Christmas-card list, but at least McConnell had the guts to answer back, calling to mind the words of the former Australia batsman and coach Bob Simpson: 'There is no doubt that the players are less respectful to umpires than they once were. Perhaps this is because the changing world we live in is less respectful to authority in general. I wonder if bowlers who are verbally happy to chirp at umpires with such cracks as "Are you blind?", "How could you make that decision?", would enjoy it if umpires, after a bad ball, said things such as "Call yourself a Test bowler?", "Hell, my grandson is more accurate than you" or "What a lot of rubbish, how on earth did you get into the Test side?"'

Even by 2005, the bleating was yet to die down. Although Tests were now officiated by two neutral umpires, one-day internationals contained one neutral and one local, which provided more than enough scope for put-upon tourists to air their grievances. Bob Woolmer was referring to Pakistan's plight in a triangular one-day series in Australia when he claimed that the decisions had gone '29–5 against us'. His explanation was tactful. 'Umpires are not cheats, I would never accuse them of that,' he said. 'The way the Australians appeal and the way the crowd supports them creates subconscious pressure on the umpires and it shows. People can say an umpire gives a decision on what he sees rather than the appeals, but I disagree. The appeal is very much a part of it. It is a very fine line.' This does not quite explain why Shane Warne continued to wring front-foot lbws out of mesmerised umpires in county cricket for so long. But as long as a home official is involved, suspicions will remain.

Let us, though, not labour under Trueman's illusion that English umpires have been the only ones not to inspire conspiracy theories. I mean, what about the Welsh? When Glamorgan won their first county championship in 1948, the decision that clinched the trophy was supposed to have been given by their compatriot Dai Davies with the words: 'That's out and we've won!' But if that could be ascribed to a spot of showmanship rather than partisanship, then Pakistan were genuinely convinced David Constant cost them victory on their trip to England in 1982. With the series all square at 1–1 going into the third and final Test at Headingley, the Pakistanis led by 219 in a low-scoring game with two second-innings wickets in hand. Then Constant ruled that their No. 10, Sikander Bakht, who had kept Imran Khan company for over an hour, had been caught by Mike Gatting at short-leg off Vic Marks. 'As was clearly evident from television pictures,' said an untypically direct *Wisden*, 'his bat missed the ball.'

On their next trip to England, in 1987, Pakistan specifically asked for Constant not to stand. The Test and County Cricket Board responded by appointing him for the second Test at Lord's and the fifth at The Oval. Five years later, again at Headingley, England were chasing 99 to square the five-Test series against Pakistan with a game to play when Graham Gooch appeared to be run out for 13. But Ken Palmer turned down the appeal – TV replays were still part of a brave new future – Gooch went on to make 37 and England won by six wickets. The snapshot of Gooch's outstretched bat, well short of the crease, was plastered all over Pakistan and taken as proof that English umpires discriminated against their heroes, a perception that was not helped by accusations of ball-tampering in 1992. At least the umpires who levelled the same charges against them fourteen years later at The Oval were from Australia and Dominica, although Darrell Hair's involvement in that instance provoked unfounded accusations of a different kind.

It's hard to escape the conclusion that the white cricket

community occasionally falls into the trap of viewing umpiring errors through the prism of race. When the long-serving Glamorgan opener Emrys Davies returned to the dressing room one day after being bowled by Frank Tyson and promptly made his mind up to become a first-class umpire, he is reported to have advertised his suitability for the job by declaring: 'I am finished. I can no longer see the ball.' We might chuckle at that, yet how many times has the alleged incompetence of Indian and Pakistani umpires been treated with just a bit too much emphasis by patronising westerners? South Africans remain convinced to this day that the only reason England beat them in 1998 was because of the crimes against geometry committed by the Pakistani umpire Javed Akhtar. And few incidents summed up the them-and-us relationship between subcontinental officials and western players better than the time Mike Gatting bumped into his old nemesis Shakoor Rana at Lord's in 2001, more than thirteen years after their finger-poking contretemps at Faisalabad had made the headlines even in Germany. True, Rana had been paid several thousand pounds by a British tabloid to fly over from Pakistan and surprise Gatting with a handshake for the benefit of a photographer. Even so, Gatting's response left little need for interpretation. 'Oh God, not you again,' he groaned, and drove off.

The era of neutral umpires has at least removed the charge of bias in Tests, but these days umpires have other concerns. For a start, TV has done them few favours. If you make a howler, the viewers at home will be treated to umpteen replays revealing exactly where the ball pitched and why the noise captured by the stump mic was a small fart rather than bat on ball. In that sense, the modern umpire is like a football goalkeeper. Do everything competently all match and hardly anyone says a word. Commit an error and suddenly small boys are laughing at you in the street. Failing that, Bob Willis will probably be mocking you on Sky. His damning assessment of the state of modern umpiring during one of those time-filling cut-backs to the studio during an England overseas Test remains a classic of its genre. 'Give me Simon Taufel and Aleem Dar any day,' seethed Bob. 'Billy Bowden's a show pony, Steve Bucknor is well past his sell-by date, and Daryl Harper's just hopeless.'

Bucknor himself sounded like one of the less plausible characters from *The X-Files* when he alleged that one or two TV producers were actually manipulating replays to make the umpires look bad. Possibly speaking from the corner of his mouth while wearing a disguise, Bucknor was quoted as saying: 'Mats have been moved, balls have disappeared, the ball hits the bat and comes up into the fielder's hands, but between the bat and the hand, no ball is found and you are told, "Sorry, we don't have that clip, we can't show it." Sometimes nothing is shown because the batsman was a key batsman and getting out at that stage would have made life very difficult for that team.' Who knows, perhaps entire Test matches have been doctored in this way. Perhaps it was actually Australia who won at Edgbaston in 2005. Perhaps Michael Vaughan doesn't really twitch his eyebrow in real-life interviews. The public deserves to know. But whether or not Bucknor was veering into the realms of Mulder and Scully, it is fair to ask if there is a more thank-less task in the world of sport. (OK, so keeping goal in handball has to be up there. Fact: Maros Kolpak, of Kolpak-cricketers fame, was a handball goalie for a German side called Östringen and remains the most obscure subject for a cricket-related interview I have ever carried out. But I digress.)

The umpire-as-scapegoat reached its nadir following the fiasco at the end of the 2007 World Cup final, when some of cricket officialdom's finest minds misinterpreted the Duckworth/Lewis regulations and insisted that the Australian team stop celebrating their victory over Sri Lanka and re-emerge into the Bridgetown darkness to bowl three more unnecessary overs. Granted, as collective aberrations go, it rubbed shoulders with the Charge of the Light Brigade. But for the ICC to respond by banning all five officials from taking part in the World Twenty20 tournament later that year in South Africa as punishment for their boo-boo was harsh in the extreme. The cricket world had moved on from Barbados. But the ICC wanted to reassert its authority after making a complete Horlicks of the sport's showcase event. Predictably, it was the umpires who got it in the neck.

Like little children, umpires are supposed to be seen but not heard. Which is partly why Simon Taufel, the highly respected Australian umpire, caused such a kerfuffle when he was overheard remarking before the start of a Test in Darwin between Australia and Bangladesh: 'Let's hope the Bangladeshis go as long as their national anthem.' Taufel's witticism earned him a ticking-off from the match referee Mike Procter and a pleasantly raised eyebrow from those who thought modern umpiring was the exclusive preserve of humourless middle-aged men. Yet if you didn't allow these people their indulgences and their misjudgements, they would probably go mad. I was once relaxing with a pint in the sleepy New Zealand town of

Hamilton, where boy-racers lend a 1950s American hicksville feel and the most exciting daily event might just be the post-kick-out-time punch-up. In walked Doug Cowie, the local umpire who earlier that year had given Andrew Flintoff out caught behind at a crucial stage of a Test at Auckland. It was, to put it politely, an absolute eye-opener for anyone who thought that Kiwi umpires only raised their finger when all three stumps were out of the ground. Flintoff had missed the ball by a foot; while Andre Adams, the bowler, stood there with an embarrassed grin on his face. To his credit, Cowie admitted to me and my drinking companions what was obvious to anyone watching at the time: that he had made a terrible mistake, referring with a sheepish smile to 'that time I screwed Flintoff'. I appreciated his honesty, but recognised the smile for what it was: an understandable need to apply humour to an incident that obviously bothered him. As Scyld Berry once wrote: 'It is one of the misapprehensions of cricket. Umpires are assumed to be merry innkeeper types, Falstaffian figures, whereas they have as many anxieties as the rest of us.'

Chief among them is the question of whether or not anyone actually gives a damn whether they exist any more. That might sound a bit drastic, but improved technology has, as Dickie Bird said, increasingly threatened to turn them into men who can count up to six (or nine, if Fidel Edwards is bowling) and who can handle sweaters, shades, caps and hats with aplomb. It is a question which divides cricket into pragmatists and romantics. Do you refer more and more decisions to the third umpire, who has recourse to TV technology, and thus detract from the importance of the two men out on the pitch? Or do you accept the inevitability of human error as an integral part of a game that ebbs and flows in any case according to the error-prone decisions of the players?

One of the romantics' favourite arguments is that things always even themselves out, as if there is a great karmic wheel stored somewhere in the Lord's pavilion which contains the same number of good and bad lbw decisions and which, when spun by three old men with beards, will dispense them equally over the course of a career. It's a bit like cricket's other piece of homespun philosophy: the law of averages. This law, often espoused by otherwise rational adults, states that a batsman luxuriating in a purple patch will sooner or later come a cropper, simply because it will be statistically freakish if the patch keeps getting purpler. It conveniently overlooks the contribution to cricket history of players like Don Bradman, who fell four runs short of averaging 100 in his Test career, and Devon Malcolm, who fell 134 short of averaging 10. And, like the karmic lbw wheel, the law of averages blithely abandons players to some strange cosmic whim. Ah well, so you missed your only ever crack at a century because the 88-year-old umpire had an insect in his eye when the bowler went up for leg-before and failed to spot the huge inside edge? Not to worry: he didn't give our No. 11 when he was plumb in front, so all's fair in love and war! What comes around goes around!

Er, not always, it doesn't. As a young Northants and England fan, I never quite got my head round the injustice of Rob Bailey being given out caught behind down the leg-side – OFF HIS HIP! – after Viv Richards's infamous Bridgetown war dance seemed to persuade umpire Lloyd Barker to raise his finger. Barker, by the way, was already en route to square-leg for the start of the next over. Bailey was given one more chance at Test level, top-scoring with 42 in Antigua, before being dropped for good – a fine reward after he had placed patriotism ahead of lucre and turned down a rebel tour of South Africa. Karmic wheel? Bailey might have another word for it.

Perhaps we shouldn't be surprised by this daily appeal to the wheel's vagaries. After all, this is a sport in which the toss of a coin carries far more weight than it does in football or rugby. Alec Stewart lost all five tosses when captain of England in Australia in 1998–99. After wrongly calling 'heads' for the fifth time, he resisted the temptation to fall to his knees in despair and pound the SCG turf, and instead inspected the guilty South African five-shilling piece, tossing it four times himself. 'It came up heads every time,' said the New Zealand match referee John Reid. It is as if luck is an integral part of cricket and we had better get used to it. But it has always struck me as unfair on the players that they should fall victim to a mistake that is obvious to everyone except the umpire who has made it.

Mark Ramprakash may have verged on the melo-dramatic after he informed Darrell Hair that 'You're messing with my career' following a caught-behind decision off his shirt during the 1998 Lord's Test against South Africa, but he had a point. Like other high-profile sports, cricket does indeed represent a career to a lot of people. Sponsors invest money in it, people pay to watch it, thousands buy papers or log on to read about it. And if that sounds dangerously close to the argument that cricket actually matters, then it is surely the case that it matters enough to use whatever technology is at your disposal. The romantics argue that the repeated referrals would waste time. Yes, they might take up a few extra minutes per day, but the extra tension they lend is ample compensation. The crowd love waiting for the big screen to reveal the result of a run-out, and the use of Hawk-Eye at Wimbledon in 2007 was a massive hit. Did the umpires feel emasculated? Was the soul of tennis sacrificed on the altar of technology? Did the competition fail to finish on time? To borrow from Maggie Thatcher: no, no, no.

It's true that technology does not always clear everything up. What far-from-bitter England fan could ever forget Simon Taufel's decision to give Michael Slater not out during the Sydney Ashes Test in 1999? Taufel, the third umpire at the time, only had two angles available to him to help him decide whether Dean Headley's direct hit from deep mid-on had ended Slater's innings on 35. But while the head-on angle appeared to rule in England's favour, the side-on view was obscured by the back of Peter Such, the England off-spinner. Common sense seemed to suggest that this didn't matter, because Slater was pretty obviously out. But Taufel pressed the green button, Slater went on to make 123 out of Australia's second-innings total of 184 (the highest percentage of runs in a completed Test innings by one batsman since the very first Test, back in 1877), and the Aussies won the series 3–1. It is also the case that referrals for catches taken centimetres off the turf have often resulted in a not-out decision because not even slo-mo replays can settle the matter one way or the other. But generally – and this is the key – technology will make far fewer errors than human beings. Point this out, though, and you are guaranteed an earful of tut-tuts from critics who might think differently if they were grabbed by the ear and tossed the white coat on the first morning of a Test.

Many people, you see, hate the thought of the umpire-as-hatstand, possibly because it detracts from the chiselled-in-stone concept of the umpire's word being final. This might be why some umpires seem more prone these days to use other means of attracting attention. Sure, David Shepherd used to hop up and down whenever the score reached 111 or one of its multiples, but then no one regarded Shep as an attention-seeker – more a lovably superstitious old so-and-so who genuinely believed that bad things would happen whenever Nelson cropped up (he once handed back the keys to the lady behind reception in an Indian hotel because the room he had been assigned was 111). Bona fide attention-seekers are characters like Billy Bowden, the New Zealand official who calls God his 'third umpire' and gives batsmen out with a bent index finger (the 'Billy hook') brought on by arthritis. And what about the South African Rudi Koertzen, who raises his left arm so slowly when giving a batsman out that they almost seem to be preparing for the next delivery by the time the arm passes beyond the horizontal? Are these foibles the dying gestures of a breed who refuse to accept their fate quietly? Or just affectations? As TV might one day say to its viewers when they throw open an lbw decision to the entire nation: you decide.

7

THE FANS

I HAVE NEVER felt more sympathy for anyone on a cricket field than Doug Cowie, and that includes the gutsy eight-year-old batting at No. 11 who made my stock delivery look like an Adam's-apple-threatening bouncer and provided me with my only wicket of the season in 2007. I mentioned in the last chapter how he gave out Andrew Flintoff in a Test at Auckland and was man enough to admit his error later on. What I didn't mention was the reaction of the crowd. Or rather, the reaction of the Barmy Army, the travelling England fans who have followed their side around the world through thin and thinner ever since they emerged as a concept in Australia in 1994–95.

Put simply, the Barmies went berserk after the dismissal was replayed on Eden Park's giant screen. At the same time, Cowie's head dropped like a guillotine when he realised, as he later explained, he had been duped by a noise he heard as ball passed bat. It was a lonely moment made worse by the baying Brits who had not spent good beer money to have the ovine-based chants with which they were taunting the New Zealand fielders interrupted by an umpiring blunder. At the risk of sounding like Oprah Winfrey, their reaction made me a touch uncomfortable, although not quite as uncomfortable as George Orwell was with English rugby fans. 'A bomb under the West car park at Twickenham on an international day,' he once wrote, 'would end fascism in England for a generation.' Most English cricket fans, by contrast, tend to err to the left of Attila the Hun, but they are passionate, noisy and occasionally drunk. And they are increasingly part of cricket's story.

That tour of New Zealand in 2001–02, my first as a journalist, was a reminder of just how important England's itinerant support had become to the image and the finances of the world game. In the match at Christchurch where Graham Thorpe made one of Test cricket's most instantly forgotten double centuries (it was hardly his fault that Nathan Astle trumped him with the innings of a lifetime), the 2,000-strong Barmy Army took up residence by themselves in one of the stands that is always full whenever the Canterbury Crusaders are playing rugby and sang as if their lives depended on it. Since the rest of the stadium was virtually empty – New Zealanders watch rugby union, one-day internationals and, if the Barmies were to be believed, sheep-shearing contests: at least, I think that's what they said – the effect was an eerie but impressive echo that reverberated around the stadium and went unchallenged by the handful of locals. By the end of the match, there was little doubt who they were, nor indeed where they came from. Without them, Lancaster Park – the biggest cricket ground in New Zealand's second biggest city, remember – would have been as lively as a Tuesday night in Napier. Love them or loathe them, the Barmy Army have never deserved to be bombed, although Christopher Martin-Jenkins, hardly the most violent man in the press box, once came close to advocating such tactics. 'Worthy souls dwell among them, no doubt,' he wrote in *The Times* at the end of England's series in South Africa in 2004–05. 'As a group, they too often demean English cricket. As Betjeman prayed of Slough: come friendly bombs and fall on them. Water bombs will do.'

Yet on and on they chant, their influence measurable by the number of spin-offs they have spawned. New Zealand, the next most self-effacing cricket nation of the lot, came up with the Beige Brigade, who wear their team's 1980s one-day strip and pine for the days of 'Ruchard' Hadlee. Misleadingly, given their preference of tipple, the strip has the colour of weak tea, but the Beige Brigade score high marks for not taking themselves too seriously and even higher marks for winding up Australians with megaphones. India's answer was the Bharat Army (*Bharat* means 'Indian' in Hindi), which hardly seemed necessary when their fans were so dedicated to the cause already. Australia came up with the Fanatics, who were little more than a yellow-garbed and embarrassingly manufactured response to the Barmies and who at least allowed England fans to maintain a feeling of superiority while their team was being stuffed by Ricky Ponting and Co in 2006–07.

One of the Barmies, Graham Cookson, even wrote a book about the experience – *Ashes to Dust* – summing up the easy contempt in which the English fans held their Aussie counterparts when he reflected on the Fanatics' efforts to match the Barmies song for song in the Test at Perth. 'The Fanatics' reply was impressive, by their own hideously low standards, a song about Ricky Ponting being magic, and wearing the baggy cap,' he condescended. 'The familiar tune was meant to be "My Old Man's a Dustman", but because it was Aussies singing everybody just shrieked their own tune, with every note sounding like a dying breath.' Who needed to win the Ashes when you could win the sing-off? As ever, England has led the way in the events that really matter – including infiltrating the end-of-series press conference at The Oval in 2005 when a beery fan who had somehow evaded the watertight security to find a seat in the back row asked a startled Michael Vaughan whether he would like to thank the England fans for their support during the course of the series. Vaughan had the good grace and common sense to say exactly that.

To these English eyes, the vast majority of travelling England fans are decent men and women who love cricket so much that they are prepared to put their lives on hold for months at a time for the privilege of being able to say (or bawl) 'I was there'. Once on a tour of Sri Lanka I interviewed several Barmies about their lifestyle and asked one of them, an employee of a bank in Leicester, how he managed to get three or four months off work every year to stand in the sun and make up puerile ditties. 'I have a very understanding manager,' he hiccuped in what might have been the understatement of the trip. This particular Barmy was a credit to his army, scrimping and saving so that he could rough it in the cheap and cheerful seaside hostelries of Hikkaduwa and watch every ball of England's nail-biting draw in the first Test at Galle. When I paid for his dinner – a delicious slap-up that cost all of £2.50 – he looked for a moment as if he might hug me, which had not been my intention. His was dedication beyond the call, and the fact that the *Guardian* had ordered an article on a potential Barmy boycott of the forthcoming trip to West Indies, where the local authorities had conjured up a ticket-price hike to make the most of the British influx, was a sign of the times: England's fans suddenly had a bit of clout.

For every good 'un, of course, there are fans you might not care to take home and meet the parents. During the 2005 Ashes, when the jingoism of the home supporters at times verged on the offensive – especially when they kept asking Jason Gillespie, who is long-haired, bearded, and has Aboriginal blood, where his caravan was – I was told a story by one of the Australian cricketers. An English fan approached him during the third Test in Manchester and simply said: '3–1'. The Australian player was nonplussed. '3–1? What do you mean?' The fan explained: 'We're going to win the Ashes 3–1.' 'OK,' replied the player. 'And what gives you the right to think you can just come up to me and behave like that?' Now it was the fan's turn to look bemused. The player continued: 'Would you approach a footballer or a rugby player and talk to him in that way?' 'Sorry, mate,' said the fan, who then desperately tried to claw back some of the moral high ground by revealing: 'I'm a cricketer too, you know.' 'So?' The fan's answers were beginning to verge on the utterly irrelevant. 'Well, I captain my club.' And then, from the player, the coup de grace: 'That doesn't change the fact that I now think you're an idiot.' It was a reminder of a basic truth that fans and, yes, journalists can often forget: the players are human beings too, especially when they are being called a Gypsy by several thousand failed stand-ups.

But revenge is nothing if not a dish best served at the temperature of Australian lager. After watching Ponting and mates put the finishing touches to their Ashes-regaining victory at Perth in December 2006, I was trudging back to my hotel through crowds of fans who seemed determined to win their private battle, even if the war was already over. The Australians sang '3–0, 3–0, 3–0', which was a reasonable point in the circumstances, while the English retaliated with a high-pitched chorus of 'Aussie, Aussie, Aussie! Oi, oi, oi!' They might have lost the cricket, but they were not going to miss an opportunity to strike at the heart of what they regarded as the macho Aussie psyche by portraying them as a bunch of squealing sheilas. The Aussies duly reasserted their maleness by baring their backsides to reveal that even in the hairy-bottom stakes, the Australians are world champions. Over the road, apparently oblivious to this high-class repartee, was a lone middle-aged England fan sitting at a bus stop. He was holding his head in his hands and muttering at the pavement. It did not seem the moment to intrude on private grief. Seconds later, an Australian fan walked past and asked him whether he had enjoyed his day. 'Er, yes thanks.' 'Good,' screamed the Aussie without a trace of irony. 'Because you won't get the Ashes back for another sixteen years!' And off he walked, triumphant in the knowledge that he had just won this gruelling battle of wits. Cricket fans are generally better behaved than their football counterparts, which might be why such vignettes feel slightly tasteless. I wanted to cross the road like some laptop-toting Samaritan and assure my compatriot that it would all be OK. The trouble was, the sixteen-year threat had a worryingly convincing ring to it.

Yet it is hard to escape the feeling that all this banter and baiting is little more than the alcohol-fuelled prejudices of those with too much time and money on their hands. Sure, the English and the Australians care, not least because bragging rights are such treasured currency in their close-knit world. But for real passion, try the sub-continent. It's all too easy to take refuge in the stereotypes which demand insane devotion from Indians and Pakistanis, especially as India is increasingly rendering stereotypes redundant by changing more quickly than almost anywhere on earth. But the reason it is so easy is that there are so many stories to back it up. Consider the tale of Sarun Sharma, a clothes seller in the parched industrial town of Jamshedpur in the north-east of India. Mr Sharma decided that the only way he could raise enough money to follow his side's fortunes – or misfortunes, as it transpired – at the World Cup in the Caribbean in 2007 was to flog one of his own kidneys for around £3,500. 'I am really serious,' he was quoted as saying. 'What's wrong with the offer? I know several people who are living with one kidney.' Having once sat through a one-day international in Mr Sharma's hometown and watched Andrew Strauss hit 74 before retiring to a saline drip in the dressing room, I wondered whether he was better off hanging onto as many organs as possible.

In Pakistan, it is not uncommon for members of the public to issue legal notices against their heroes in an American-style atmosphere of litigious resentment. When Shoaib Akhtar left the action during a Test against India at Rawalpindi in 2004 complaining of wrist and back pain, subsequent scans struggled to pinpoint the exact nature of the problem. Whispers that his wrist and back were not actually as troublesome as he had made out grew when Shoaib headed for Mumbai to shoot a commercial and have a jolly night out on the town. For one fan of Pakistan, Mr Babar Ali, this was too much to take, so he promptly instructed his lawyer to file for a claim of almost £1m for the emotional torment Shoaib had put him through. He expected it to be paid within fifteen days. 'Akhtar pretended injury and let the whole nation down and then rubbed salt on the wounds with his off-field actions,' said Mr Ali's lawyer, who might not have been able to believe his luck. I suspect Shoaib is still in possession of the money.

Cricket matters more to the subcontinent for a variety of reasons, but I imagine I might feel the same degree of indignation as Mr Ali if my experience of watching the game involved queueing for hours in the sun to pay for the privilege of parking my backside on a concrete step for the day. My first experience of cricket in India came at the Wankhede Stadium in Mumbai, a giant creaking edifice whose name – should your comedy routine be falling flat – is guaranteed a titter from an audience after a couple of glasses of wine. It was there, in early 2002, that Andrew Flintoff decided to take his shirt off after bowling Javagal Srinath and whirl it round his head like a cheerleader's routine gone horribly wrong. The size of the crowd was staggering enough for someone used to the peace and quiet of the county circuit. But two moments stood out. The first came when Darren Gough had the local boy Sachin Tendulkar caught behind for just 12, sparking the kind of disquieting peace you find on a misty Sunday morning in an English graveyard; the second when Sourav Ganguly, then the captain, was booed at the post-match reception by angry Mumbaikars who had spent several hours watching in cramped conditions as their heroes blew it in a crucial one-day match for the umpteenth time. Through the binoculars, I could swear Ganguly's eyes had moistened. Or perhaps it was just the heat.

Four years later, I covered a one-day international in a town called Faridabad, about an hour's drive south of Delhi, where hundreds of fans who had bought legitimate tickets were not allowed into the ground because others who had bought theirs on the black market had pinched their seats. When the aggrieved supporters caused an angry bottleneck at the stadium entrance, they were baton-charged by the local police. It was a cowardly manoeuvre and left a small girl in hospital. The response of Faridabad's district commissioner hardly helped matters. 'Sometimes people need to be disciplined,' he said, presumably whacking himself over the head with his own lathi.

The next game, in sultry Goa, provided a more stomach-churning example of the hardships sometimes endured by followers of the Indian game. A colleague's sister was travelling around the country with three friends, and spending a day at the cricket to watch another England defeat seemed like the obvious thing to do. Facilities at the Margao stadium were rudimentary, but for a handful of rupees the girls found they were able to buy a tasty carton of rice. Or so they thought. A couple of hours later, one of them went in search of a toilet and happened to walk past an open door. Inside was a man with a big broom. He had casually gathered up all the half-eaten containers of rice and poured the contents onto the floor. Now, he was sweeping up the rice, mixed appetisingly with dust, grit, grime and possibly the odd cockroach, and redistributing it into containers for sale to the unwitting public. Next time you're in Goa, plump for the naan bread.

Later in the series we flew to Guwahati in the state of Assam, that forgotten part of India to the east of Bangladesh and the south of Bhutan. There are few more unlikely venues in the world game and it's almost worth a visit just for the novelty factor. When our coach arrived in what remains the grubbiest town I have ever watched cricket in – just pipping Northampton – the streets suddenly became lined with locals convinced that we shambling hacks were in fact the England cricket team. Slightly fearful of being mobbed as our coach pulled up outside our hotel, we sent out Mike Walters of the *Daily Mirror* – a man whose many qualities do not include looking like an international sportsman – to thank the 'good people of Guwahati on behalf of the British press for their kind welcome'. This so nonplussed the locals that we somehow forced our way into the hotel, shaking a few hands on the way and explaining that, no, they really didn't want my autograph, and, no, there wasn't much point in our posing for photographs because we genuinely weren't Kevin Pietersen or Andrew Flintoff or even, for the more mature among us, Duncan Fletcher.

But who could blame them? India had played seven one-day internationals at Guwahati's Nehru Stadium (there are five Nehru Stadiums in India, each apparently oblivious to the other four) since losing to West Indies there in December 1983. And they had played none at all since beating Zimbabwe in March 2002. The only thing was, it had been raining in the days leading up to the match. And when it rains in Guwahati, it doesn't hold back. The sky turns an apocalyptic greyish-green and you can hardly see for stair rods. Come the day of the match, the sun was shining, but the pitch was still far too sodden to think about play. A large crowd turned up anyway and waited and waited and waited. If a tannoy system had been in operation, they would have been told that the down-pours of the previous few days had rendered the outfield unplayable, no matter how scorching the sun was now. But the lack of information started to eat away at the locals. They began pulling apart fences and hurling bottles onto the outfield, at which point the police decided to join in. What followed was not the kind of thing you see on a lazy Friday morning in the Ladies' Pavilion at New Road. The police fired tear gas over the heads of the fans, then lathi-charged them for good measure as they fled en masse for the one available exit. As one officer lay motionless on the outfield after being hit by a flying brick, two men were grabbed at random from the crowd and beaten absolutely senseless by the constabulary. Dixon of Dock Green would have shaken his head sadly. In fact, had I been in the two men's position, I would probably have asked for my money back.

Writing all this, I'm a bit concerned that I sound like the archetypal patronising Englishman, leaning back in his comfy seat at Lord's with his copy of the *Daily Telegraph* and smugly announcing, like the Major in *Fawlty Towers*, that 'Boycott got a century!' I am not that man (I prefer the *Guardian*). For no place feels more alive to the cricket lover than India – a feeling that was reinforced when I went back for the first two weeks of the Indian Premier League in 2008 – and I still get goosebumps when I recall the roar that went up in the Delhi crowd when Gautam Gambhir and Virender Sehwag walked out at the Feroz Shah Kotla to kick-start the one-day series against England two years earlier. It was excitement mixed with fervour mixed with nationalism, and it was thrillingly unique. Yet at the same time these fans were rewarded for their loyalty by not being allowed to bring their own water into a packed ground, the worry being that they would end up throwing the empty bottles onto the pitch. When Soumya Bhattacharya, an Indian cricket fan turned writer, visited Lord's for the first time in 1993, he was impressed by what he found. 'For someone who had grown up watching cricket on the subcontinent, I was struck by how *comfortable* the whole experience could be, how civilised and pleasurable,' he wrote in 2007 on *Cricinfo*. 'I associated watching the game with eking out eight inches on a concrete bench for my bum, queuing endlessly for food and water, being pelted with an orange or worse if I stood up to applaud. Here there were sumptuous lunch hampers, there was wine and beer, as much space as I wanted for myself, a book for the breaks, and the patter of measured applause. Everyone seemed to be having a good time. Sometimes the cricket seemed only incidental.' It's not better or worse. It's just different. And I wouldn't have it any other way.

But another type of Indian fan is emerging, one that is less likely to be caught by the coppers in a Guwahati scrum or walloped over the head with a stick of bamboo in Faridabad. We have been hearing about the rise of the moneyed Indian middle classes for a few years now, and every trip to Mumbai confirms the impression of a country where the rich are getting richer, even if the poor are heading in the other direction. An off-shoot of this new money is that the Indians suddenly have the time and the funds to do what the English have been doing for years and follow their team around the globe. One of the strangest parts of being in the Caribbean for the World Cup in 2007 was the sight of middle-aged Indian men hanging around hotel lobbies as they wondered what to do with their day – beach or, er, beach? – following India's early exit. The rooms had been booked well in advance in expectation of India's involvement in the Super Eights, but their team had not obliged. Yet here they were, wearing the middle-class cricket fan's touring costume of choice: polo shirt, fashionably long Bermuda shorts, expensive flip-flops, shades perched extraneously on their head. Many of them were part of the Indian diaspora in the US, but the trend was unmistakable enough: Indians had the money and they were starting to put it to good use.

It was not the only indication that the profile of the average Indian fan was changing. The deference of old had given way to a whiff of entitlement. They stood around in large groups and made lots of noise. They treated the hotel staff with a casualness that bordered on arrogance. They complained about trifles. They wanted, it was easy to imagine, their pillows plumped, their cocktails cheap and their exchange rate preferential. In short, they behaved in the same way as a certain type of England fan has been behaving for years. I had never quite been able to grasp the traditional accusations about the arrogant English before, although I may have winced once or twice when a colleague lapsed into old-school colonialism to get his way with an overly obliging Indian. But now, liberated by a greater degree of objectivity, I could see that the more self-satisfied English cricket fan must have been regarded over the years by his overseas host as a necessary evil: good for the economy, bad for the peptic ulcer.

If the travelling Indian fan was a changing beast, so too, it seemed, were some of the Pakistanis. Very few of them leave their homeland to watch Pakistan play abroad, although Abdul Jalil, who sports a white W.G. Grace beard and is known to his compatriots as Chacha ('Uncle'), has become such a fixture wherever his side turns out that he even draws a small salary from the Pakistan Cricket Board. But when England visited in 2005–06, still light-headed after their Ashes-winning celebrations, they met with the kind of response that would have been unthinkable in the days when Mike Gatting and Shakoor Rana had their disagreement. Thanks to some visionary thinking from Chacha, many members of the Multan crowd were waving not only the green-and-white crescented flag of Pakistan but the Union Jack as well. Several teenagers were wearing England one-day outfits; some even had the St George's cross painted on their faces. Imagine an Englishman arriving at an Ashes Test at Lord's wearing goggles and a swimming cap and brandishing a blow-up kangeroo. Yet here they were, young Pakistan fans cheering on the team who had just seen off the Aussies.

So much for the differences. For those who take the philosophical view that, deep down, we're all the same, the realisation that all cricket fans are bound by a common outlook is reassuring. The fact that this common outlook manifests itself in superstition is neither here nor there. The truth is that cricket does weird things to all of us. During a stint at the keyboard for the *Guardian*'s over-by-over coverage of a one-day game against Sri Lanka, I happened to mention that Marcus Trescothick was playing rather well. Two overs later he was out. And not long after that, my inbox was full of emails from readers who were only half-joking when they accused me of costing Trescothick his wicket. It was chaos theory gone mad.

'Lawrence, you TOOL!' wrote Richard Marsden, who was among the more restrained correspondents. 'You ****ing jinx,' began Roland Marshall, who was more typical. 'Well done, Mr Booth, you just couldn't resist it could you? Why oh why do you have to tempt fate at the most inappropriate times? Are you a Sri Lankan (or worse, an Australian) in disguise?' Patrick Kemp took a similar tack: 'Booth, you are a moron. More of the "dangerous-looking Sri Lankan attack" and less of the "Bell could post a big score here", please.' Jonny Martin sensed my soothsaying skills might be of use to his financial situation. 'Nice predicting, Boothy,' he wrote. 'Could you just predict for me that I definitely won't get a 10% pay rise? It's the only way I can see it happening . . .' The idea that Trescothick was actually the one at fault for losing his wicket seemed not to have occurred. No, I had tempted fate, and in the self-contained world of cricket this was a crime punishable by fifty-three rude emails.

It is the same everywhere. Players refuse to move seats if two of their team-mates are putting together a partnership out in the middle. Batsmen insist on putting their left pad on first, or their sun hat or their Noddy and Big Ears jockstrap. Bowlers actually believe it makes a difference if they turn to the left or the right at the top of their mark. Commentators talk about the kiss of death after they have just praised someone for a gorgeous cover-drive, except for Geoff Boycott, who says 'You'll never get him out' without the slightest doubt in his own mind that he is absolutely correct. And some fans actually place money on the game, in defiance of Richie Benaud's insistence that you should never bet on anything with two legs. One fan, an MCC member, once placed £100 at odds of 1000–1 on the top four Australian batsmen all scoring centuries against England at Lord's in 1993. Mark Taylor, Michael Slater and David Boon duly obliged, only for Mark Waugh to be bowled between his legs by Phil Tufnell for 99. One run cost the man £100,000. Hell, it's almost enough to make you superstitious.

8

The Media

THESE DAYS – at the risk of coming across all Fred Trueman – the fans are so spoiled for media choice that they really *do* know what's going off out there. Way back when I was still harbouring dreams of opening the batting for Northamptonshire Seconds on a flat one at Wantage Road, the only socially acceptable way of finding out how quickly England's latest collapse was progressing was to switch on the TV or radio. Even then you risked being confronted with the 3.10 from Ascot or the shipping forecast. If you wanted to salvage what remained of your credibility, Ceefax was to be watched with the lights out and the curtains drawn. But mobile phones and the internet have changed everything. A friend who was stuck at a christening managed to follow the blood-curdling final stages of the Trent Bridge Ashes Test in 2005 by repeatedly SMS-ing a hassled hack in the press box. The following summer I braved strange looks at Zurich airport to use WAP technology and watch Kevin Pietersen reverse-slap Muttiah Muralitharan for six at Edgbaston. And there may never have been more mobile phones glued to ears at a cricket match than during the chaos of the Darrell Hair Test against Pakistan in 2006, when the information provided by the stadium announcers was so threadbare that phoning a friend was a far better way of finding out what the hell was going on. Miss all that, of course, and you can probably catch up on YouTube.

Back in 1990, when the BBC failed to broadcast the tuck to backward square-leg for a single that made Graham

Gooch the first Englishman to score a triple hundred in a Test for twenty-five years because they had gone to 'the racing' (two words that have sent a shiver down my spine ever since), standards were different. It was considered the height of innovation if the camera drew slowly back from the action at 12.55 p.m. as Tony Lewis gravely informed viewers that we would now be going to the local news. This generally went without a hitch, but when Richard Illingworth bowled the West Indian opener Phil Simmons in 1991 with his first ball in Test cricket at around 12.54, the cameraman zoomed back in as if he had just been electrocuted. Innocent days. Now, you can barely move for gizmos: Hawk-Eye, the red strip running from wicket to wicket which makes smart-arse umpires of us all, the Snickometer, the Hot Spot, and – most intriguing of the lot – Mark Nicholas's extra-long-lasting hair gel. Analysis is everywhere, increasingly so in the daily newspapers, which are forced to stray away from the realms of mere match reporting because fans are so clued up: by the time they pick up the following morning's rag, the essentials of Kevin Pietersen's latest celebratory wave of the bat towards Jessica Taylor have already been done to death on the web, as well as absorbed, digested and regurgitated by supporters who demand a lot more from their correspondent than a tally of fours, sixes, balls and minutes.

Originality is fast becoming the *sine qua non*, but for newspapermen used to producing copy that retains its freshness over next morning's kippers, the internet makes life hard. (I say newspaper*men* only because there are so few women in cricket writing. When Stephen Fry's General Melchett tells Hugh Laurie's George that trying to rescue Blackadder from behind German lines would be 'as pointless as trying to teach a woman the value of a good forward defensive stroke', he was summing up an attitude that has lingered long beyond the First World War. Female under-representation in the press box remains a scandal.) Anyway, the internet. Online over-by-over coverage keeps work-shy fans up to date with the latest news of other readers' love lives, best-man-speech dilemmas, and – when not much else is happening – the cricket. Match reports appear on the internet almost before the fast bowlers have climbed cursing into their ice baths. Blogs sprout like chickenpox, and in turn generate a whole host of comments from readers, some of them occasionally relating to the article under which they appear. One or two per batch tend to be abusive (sports writers provoke envy: that's my explanation and I'm sticking to it); a few are genuinely enlightening. But from a writer's point of view the whole experience is as unnerving as facing Murali on a Colombo turner: not only is your professional competence placed in the cyberspatial stocks for the whole world to mull over, but the public's rotten tomatoes now leave visible imprints too. A shower of verbal veg has become the journalist's equivalent of a cricketer being booed. We all get judged now, including the players themselves. When Michael Vaughan denied using the word 'Fredalo' during an interview with the *Guardian* in 2007, the newspaper responded by posting an audio version of his chat with the journalist on its website. These days, the old claim that 'I was quoted out of context, guv' lies on shakier ground.

But if the relationship between writers and readers has entered its fraughtest phase yet, then that between cricketers and their press-box tormentors has rarely been less than sensitive. The 1948 *Wisden* obituary of Warwick Armstrong contains the following observation: 'Like many cricketers, after retiring from active participation in the game, Armstrong wrote for the Press, and his caustic Test criticisms created ill-feeling of a kind which should not be associated with cricket.' Once you have stopped chuckling at the assertion that cricket, like a maiden aunt, should be shielded from the pernicious effects of 'ill-feeling', it is worth remembering that Armstrong's career in journalism took place in relatively naive pre-war days. Since then the players' feelings towards the press have shifted from love-hate to dislike-hate, with plenty of scope for further deterioration.

When Andrew Flintoff sat down for yet another press conference in Perth in December 2006, his whispered mutter to the ECB media-relations officer was picked up by more than one Dictaphone: 'Get me out of here as quickly as possible.' It was Flintoff's way of saying what Hunter S. Thompson had expressed in less succinct terms in his gonzo-journalism novel *Fear and Loathing in Las Vegas*. 'The press is a gang of cruel faggots,' he mused 'Journalism is not a profession or a trade. It is a cheap catch-all for fuckoffs and misfits – a false doorway to the backside of life, a filthy piss-ridden little hole nailed off by the building inspector, but just deep enough for a wino to curl up from the sidewalk and masturbate like a chimp in a zoo-cage.' It's a good job Thompson never made it into the Lord's media centre on a rainy day, although he would have applauded the gesture by a former England batsman who once found himself stuck in an elevator with a journalist from his local paper. Without saying a word, the player unzipped his flies, pulled out his manhood and urinated down the startled hack's leg. 'What was that for?' he shrieked. 'You've been pissing all over me for years so I thought I'd let you know how it feels,' came the reply.

Not all cricketers, it is true, would have gone quite as far as Thompson or the penny-spending cricketer. Len Hutton, for one, was far removed from the masturbating-winos school of thought when he was captaining England in the 1950s. 'I believe that cricketers,' he wrote, 'like anyone else in the public eye, must be prepared to accept praise and criticism with equal grace, not allowing the one to cause a need for a larger county cap, or the other to represent anything more than a friendly rap on the knuckles, which, even if undeserved, never hurt anybody.' In a chapter entitled 'Cricketers and the Press' in his 1956 book *Just My Story*, Hutton even described press conferences as 'almost useless' – not because they generate more clichés than a Californian self-help manual, but because 'Newspapermen do not want to be told collectively the same thing; each hopes for something different and as each has to satisfy a particular editor, I hold that the captain should try to give each man individual consideration.' To a generation of journos anaesthetised by the mind-numbing effects of coached soundbites, Hutton's sensitivity sounds almost too good to be true. Nearly fifty years later Michael Vaughan, another Yorkshire and England captain, was more guarded when it came to commenting on the refusal of Robert Mugabe's government to allow several British reporters into Zimbabwe to cover England's one-day series. Whatever you think of the British press, went the gist of Vaughan's lukewarm plea, they must be allowed in. Just make sure the beds aren't too comfortable and why not arrange a beer with the Zimbabwean police while you're at it, he didn't need to add.

Yet for all the increasing antagonism, the fact is that players and journalists enjoy a grudging symbiosis. The players are encouraged to think of themselves as very important by journalists who render their every burp in loving shorthand, while the journalists begin to believe that what they are writing matters too, mainly because they are in a job that many thirty-something males regard as the closest thing to heaven on earth. The two groups are part of a conspiracy theory in which it suits both to maintain the pretence that cricket really is worth the amount of space it gets in the papers when the football season is over. And nowhere is this pretence more regularly played out than in press conferences, especially the ones at the end of a day's play in a Test match. To call these charades a game would be an understatement along the lines of branding the 2007 World Cup in the Caribbean a fiasco, for there are strict rules and regulations to adhere to. Since the player 'up for quotes' will either have scored runs or taken wickets that day, matters tend to kick off with a none-too-taxing 40 mph half-volley on leg-stump: 'Pleased with that, Michael/ Freddie/KP?' I await the moment when the response, delivered with the deadest of pans, goes: 'What do you think, you quotes-mad inadequate? That I wanted to get a first-baller/bowl like a constipated hippo?' It is yet to happen, but I will cheer when it does.

On bad days, journalists might roll over and have their tummies tickled for something as profound as a cliché. When Graham Gooch was asked how he felt after that triple hundred against India, he exclusively revealed that he was 'OK'. But the blood-out-of-a-stone prize for mute magnificence during my limited quotes-gathering existence goes to Glamorgan's Alex Wharf, a taciturn Bradfordian who ended up winning the man-of-the-match award on his international debut after removing Sourav Ganguly, V.V.S. Laxman and Rahul Dravid in his first three overs. 'It couldn't have gone much better than that, Alex!' 'Ay, it were all right.' 'You must be delighted!' 'Yeah, not bad.' 'Did you ever think you'd get rid of such an illustrious trio so early on your debut?' 'No, not really.' 'Why is your nickname Gangster?' 'Best leave that one in the past.' 'Is your name Alex Wharf?' 'Might be.' Or words to that effect. On and on it went, each monosyllable more defiant than the last, and all the while Michael Vaughan, sitting to Wharf's right, doing his best to suppress a chuckle. After fifteen minutes of this life-draining torture, an Indian television reporter cracked. 'Since Alex Wharf clearly has no interest in answering our questions,' she raged, 'I will address this one to Michael Vaughan . . .' There would have been a sharp intake of breath had everyone not fallen asleep.

Generally, though, things progress along predictable lines. In fact, they have been progressing along predictable lines for quite some time now. Here's Frank Keating recalling a typical press conference from the England tour of the West Indies in 1980–81: 'All the old rhubarb – "There's more pressure on them than us" . . . "Everyone says that we have a chance now the great man, Vivvy, is not playing, but even without him we do not underestimate them . . ." and so on and so forth. You felt you were at a minor manager's interview before the third round of the Cup which, as we all know ad tedium is a "great leveller" and "it's just another game for us, and they'll have to do all the worrying".' As Vic Marks once wrote of Inzamam-ul-Haq's press pronouncements: 'Much Urdu about nothing'. Shakespeare, alas, it is not.

Of course, the more worldly-wise players – the wily Hutton included – understand that a harmonious relationship with the media can work both ways. As Hutton implied, a journalist's first loyalty is to his editor, and while we would all like to think of ourselves as fearless seekers of the truth, it's fair to say that the truth becomes a woolly concept when it's a matter of decoding the latest soundbites or analysing Stuart Clark's line and length. No, stories and angles are what matter, and preferably stories and angles where a strong headline writes itself. Mike Atherton, now a highly respected writer and broadcaster himself, didn't give a pint of Tetley's for this nuance when he was in charge of a poor England team, and was christened Captain Grumpy by hacks who grew fed up with his default shrug of the shoulders. But Nasser Hussain understood the game perfectly, and the media loved him for it. After England had beaten Australia at Headingley in 2001, a result that would never have occurred had the Australian stand-in captain Adam Gilchrist not generously declared in the hope of setting up the possibility of a series whitewash, Atherton turned to Hussain on the dressing-room balcony and said: 'You jammy bastard.' Hussain responded with a wink and a reference to the poor saps in the media. 'I'll keep conning them for a while yet.' Similarly, when the New Zealand captain Stephen Fleming opined that his Australian counterpart Steve Waugh was 'very good at using the media for his own ends', it was as much a compliment as an insult.

As with Andy Caddick's temples, grey areas abound.

Because however much grown journalists wail openly when Monty Panesar tells them he wants to 'keep it simple' and 'hit the right areas', they must bear some of the blame themselves. As we saw with the Vaughan/Fredalo shemozzle, the players' traditional lament when they are quoted as saying they will give less than 110 per cent or they are underestimating the vastly improved United Arab Emirates is that their words have been 'taken out of context'. This covers a multitude of sins, of which the most common is that they did indeed insult the UAE and are now regretting providing the plucky Middle East outfit with a ready-made team talk. The result of all this is that most players have retreated into their shells/bubbles/caves (delete according to latest media-training manual) and emerge only to state the bleeding obvious. Things seemed to go wrong in England some time during the mid-1980s, when scores of news journalists – they're the proper journalists who generally report on things that matter, like war, famine and Britney Spears – were assigned to England tours, ostensibly to convey the misery of our boys' latest thrashing, but in actual fact to ascertain how many beds a certain all-rounder had broken at the last count. Cricket correspondents seethed at being tarred with the same brush as these tabloid scufflers, but the die was cast. Players gave less away, so journalists had to be more inventive with the scraps they were tossed. And so the players felt besieged, and the journalists felt deprived. If the whole process were not so knuckle-gnawingly tedious, it might be described as a vicious circle.

When, in 2006, the *Times* columnist Libby Purves wrote about politicians, she might, in a weird parallel universe, have had cricketers in mind too: 'It is hypocritical of media commentators to complain about politicians disguising their rich humanity. We, ourselves, have done this to them. It is our fault. We mock, we sketch-write, we bestow cruelly apt nicknames, we force them to iron out everything that does not fit in with our template of middling ordinariness. If they speak robustly and wittily we accuse them of "gaffes". If they admit that they don't know something – anything – we pour contumely on them. The unforeseen result of this British approach to political reporting is a toxic twin track. Either MPs are ambitious and become carefully dull and skilled in meaningless circumlocution; or else they accept that they won't ever make it to the top and become clowns . . .' If Panesar fits into the first category, then I can think of countless others who nestle snugly into the second. But perhaps the rub lies in what we write. As Frances Edmonds noted: 'When England is doing well, and the press is busily filing laudatory encomiums of often quite excessive and unctuous praise, then the player–press boat seems to rock along quite smoothly. When the team is failing badly, however, the media worm inevitably turns, and many a player's hubris and carefully massaged ego is loath to take the slightest hint of personal criticism. It is then that the affair turns sour.'

Edmonds was on to something, having observed at first hand the way the players began to regard the press as the devil's spawn during England's tour of the West Indies in 1985–86. But her observation raises another question: can the media actually affect what takes place on the field of play? Can they, by what they write or broadcast, alter the mood of the players to the extent that runs are scored and wickets taken which would otherwise have gone down as dot-balls? The sight of Nasser Hussain, turning towards the Lord's media centre and gesticulating furiously at the 'No. 3' on the back of his blue England one-day shirt after scoring a hundred against India in 2002, suggests that the old line about players never reading the papers is an economy with the truth. And, no, looking at pictures in the *Daily Star* doesn't count.

In fact, the evidence leaves little doubt that this kind of self-consciousness has always been intact. In his tour report following England's hammering in Australia in 1950–51, the captain Freddie Brown drew a simplistic correlation between the poison in journalists' pens and the travails of his own team. 'I do believe that if these cricket writers were to encourage rather than write down England, our side would show up better on the field,' he fulminated. Bertie Buse, an all-rounder for Somerset either side of the war, once failed to budge from his position at long-on after the ball had been lofted in his general direction. 'Why the hell didn't you go for that catch?' spluttered a team-mate. 'Oh, it was a bit awkward,' came the reply. 'And if you put one down, they always put it in the paper.' More recently, Steve James admitted in his autobiography that he used to wonder how the broadsheet writers covering one of his many epics at Colwyn Bay would craft their prose, specifically about him. 'What adjectives would they use to describe me?' he wrote. 'That always fascinated me, some-times even enticing me to attempt to play as described – say phlegmatically, or studiously, or even fluently.' James, now a distinguished journalist himself, may have pondered the question more readily than some of his less literary team-mates, but the snippet is telling. Why else did the South African team that toured England in 2003 hire the

broadcaster and former India opener Ravi Shastri to brief
them on the behaviour of the British press if they were not
concerned that words could hurt them? 'We are fully aware
of the poison pens that are being readied ahead of our
arrival,' said their captain, Graeme Smith, with appropriate
melodrama. As things turned out, the media spent a lot of
the summer writing about Smith's double hundreds.

Of course, the musings of the fourth estate can have
the opposite effect too. And if the hackneyed line about so-
and-so proving his critics wrong sounds suspiciously like a
self-obsessed conceit of the press, then there have been
moments when what appears in print really does come
back to haunt its perpetrator. The most hilarious example
in recent times came on England's Ashes tour of 1986–87,
when Martin Johnson, a superbly funny writer who earned
the nickname 'Scoop' because he never lets a story get in
the way of a high-class joke, declared in the *Independent* that
there were only three things wrong with Mike Gatting's
team. They couldn't bat, they couldn't bowl, and they
couldn't field. England won 2–1 and Johnson entered
folklore.

In fact, gaffes – a word you only ever seem to read in
the papers – might just be the pressman's most productive
route to fame and fortune. I've always wondered whether
the cynicism found in sports writers – greater, it seems,
than in other branches of journalism – stems from the
knowledge that, deep down, they are writing about nothing
more than a game. And in cricket's case a pretty strange
one. 'Man hits ball and runs,' jokes a friend when trying to
guess my take on a day's play, and I have had many eureka
moments when the futility of what I do has left me feeling
dizzy and in need of a stiff drink. 'Anyone who has worked

in Fleet Street,' wrote Julian Henry in the *Guardian* in 2005, 'knows that sports writers are a moody bunch, embittered because they've been condemned to a life of inconsequence on the back pages, and this means they don't take kindly to outsiders no matter who they work for.' To which I say: who asked you, loser?

In that respect, cricket writers are no less guilty of inhabiting a Neverland of make-believe and eternal puerility than the players. And it makes them long to be taken seriously. During England's tour of West Indies in 1980–81, the press opted not to attend a warm-up match because they were waiting around for the resolution of the Jackman Affair. Robin Jackman, a fast bowler with South African connections, had been barred from entering Guyana by the local government, which was cracking down hard on any links with the apartheid regime. It was a proper news story and the *Guardian*'s Frank Keating was quite excited. 'We were selfishly pleased to have missed the trip to sugar cane country,' he declared, 'for here we could at least seem important, sitting as it were at the apparent heart of things, and only hearing of another humiliation for England from a second-hand source.' It sounds wrong, but I can empathise. The favourite week of my journalistic life so far came in the aftermath of the abandoned Oval Test against Pakistan, when the story opened itself up and invited you to follow your nose – the journalist's second-most crucial body part after his liver. Usually in cricket, the story is a self-contained entity, taking place before your eyes on the field as you sip tea and eat cakes. But the Darrell Hair story required more than that: man hits ball, runs, and umpire calls it all off. Or something like that.

Nicholas Tomalin, the British journalist killed in the

Syrian Golan Heights in 1973, believed the three qualities a reporter needs are 'rat-like cunning, a plausible manner, and a little literary ability', but these days it helps to have a smattering of humour too. Controversially, the cricket reporter – a breed that has always fancied itself as more rounded than some of its sports-writing colleagues – is being called upon to deal with matters that are even more irrelevant than the cricket itself. The apogee of this off-the-wall approach is the over-by-over coverage that is now commonplace on several of Britain's national newspaper websites. The interest I declared earlier, may as well be reiterated here: I have spent many hours – some of them ungodly – sitting in front of a TV screen in the offices of the *Guardian*'s website writing about England's latest travails so that users from the Andes to Zambia can find out the latest score. More than that, they can indulge in a self-consciously outré form of banter by sending in their own musings for publication alongside the insights into the cricket. The result is a weird but captivating mixture of reportage and wackiness that has proved so popular it has been replicated by the BBC, *The Times* and the *Daily Telegraph*, where they have even managed to crack a few gags. It is an area in which, for once, cricket feels ahead of the game.

Writing the over-by-over coverage helps you gauge the mood of the average fan (or at least, as a couple of *Daily Mail*-reading acquaintances put it, of the average muesli-eating, sandal-wearing, newspaper-recycling Guardianista). England fans, it becomes clear after sifting through an inbox groaning with their observations, are a wry, dry bunch who have learned to take refuge from the misery of following the national side in the 1990s by treating failure like a long-lost friend. This may be because some of them, especially those you encounter on the graveyard shifts that involve getting up at 3 a.m. to cover a Test on the sub-continent, live abroad and lap up anything that reconnects them with leather, willow and pastures green.

In that sense, a deprived diaspora of cricket-loving Brits comes as close to defining the typical over-by-over reader as anything. But there are also thousands of bored office workers across the UK who have developed a faintly obsessional, and in some cases narcissistic, relationship with their F5 key as they wait for the latest *bon mot* to fill their screens. More than one reader claims to have lost a job because the boss has spotted too much over-by-over activity. And then there are the non-English readers: the Australians who enjoy causing trouble, the Indians who come up with statistics that even Bill Frindall would reject on the grounds of obscurity, and the South Africans who miss the irony. 'Lawrence, am I mad?' wrote one reader. 'A now-Kiwi ex-Pom, crouched over a computer in Auckland, "watching" England trying to win a Test match . . . in writing.' Yes, that pretty well sums it up.

The OBO – let's use the acronym its aficionados know it by – kicked off in earnest during the 2002–03 Ashes series, when gallows humour kept me going through the long nights as England went down to a 4–1 defeat. But it was not until the 2005 Ashes series that it indisputably attained cult status (and even spawned a book: yes, a book of highlights of the musings of someone watching England on the TV interspersed with gags from people who were reading these musings. Needless to say, it worked). And it was in the bleak months that followed the high of England's defeat of Australia that the OBO even coined a new term: the Johnny Come Lately, or – this being the sport of lbw, CMJ and FEC – the JCL. What emerged as I opened emails at the crack of dawn and tried manfully to listen to Bob Willis's latest outburst above the noise of the latest fire-alarm test was that cricket fans who had stuck with England over the years resented the new breed of fan who had leapt aboard the Ashes bandwagon and were now dropping off, one by one, as the team made a mess of things in Pakistan.

'I am a Johnny Come Lately,' confessed one brave reader, 'and now I will be a Johnny Go Lately too. I am only interested if England win.' Proper England fans, countered the stalwarts, take maths-defying collapses on the chin. 'Do those JCLs that still follow the OBO do so out of cricketing interest?' asked one outraged member of the old school. 'Or because it's infinitely more interesting reading the ramblings of fellow bored desk-jockeys than actually working?' And with that he presumably went back to polishing the leather patches on the elbows of his tweed jacket. One or two, though, were alive to the trend. 'Is it me,' began one email, 'or do this morning's "hardcore" cricket fans seem inordinately bitter about the fact that the Ashes may have introduced a new generation to cricket? I get the feeling that they're all secretly delighted: England are losing, you can all be miserable again, you've got your sport back. Happy now?!'

To be in touch with the mental machinations of the fans is a fascinating process. But it can be disquieting too. Until I sat down for OBO duty for England's tour of Pakistan in 2005–06, my most unnerving brush with members of the public had come during a night out in Manchester when I found myself chatting to a group of worse-for-wear fans about the day's play at the Test. 'What do you do then, mate?' one of them asked. 'I'm a journalist.' The music stopped and tumbleweed rolled into view from nowhere in particular. 'Who do you write for?' asked another. This wasn't heading in a direction I was comfortable with. 'The *Guardian*,' I ventured, suddenly feeling like a petty criminal. 'They're shit,' exclaimed a third, at which point I turned round and walked off without another word. Seconds later I felt a hand on my collar. It was the ugliest member of the group, and possibly the drunkest. 'You boys are scum,' he pointed out from a couple of inches away, covering my specs in a thick mist of breathy Boddingtons. 'I'm going to take you outside, stamp on your glasses and beat the crap out of you.' Christ, I thought. If that's what he'd like to do to a *Guardian* cricket writer, what plans might he have in store for a *News of the World* gossip columnist? A vat of boiling oil? A branding iron? We were saved such speculation by one of his less-pissed mates, who prised the baboon off me with a 'Leave it, he ain't worth it'. The feeling was mutual, although my membership of the Cricket Writer's Club precluded violence.

But that was kid's stuff. Throughout England's tour of Pakistan, my inbox was peppered by emails from a reader with an Indian name who discerned racism in my every comment and at one point blamed me personally for the Amritsar massacre of 1919, when British troops fired on a crowd of unarmed civilians. It was a hard one to argue. On another occasion, I criticised a decision by the third umpire that happened to go against England. An email landed from a character calling himself Imran Khan. It began. 'Lawrence Booth, you are a total c**t.' It concluded with, 'I hope you enjoy this fine England win right into the path of a speeding bus,' and – the best bit – signed off with a cheery 'kind regards'. England went on to lose and I steered clear of the outside of the pavement on the way home. Sometimes interactivity can go too far.

And yet, the evidence suggests that the OBO is on to a winner. Love 'em or feel completely indifferent to 'em, the JCLs are symptomatic of a new group of fans for whom cricket has become more than a dusty sport played in sepia for the benefit of the old school. If the Ashes alerted them to the potential cricket has to be the most viscerally disturbing game of them all, then the OBO has helped keep the interest of a decent number of them by demonstrating that cricket coverage need not be all about describing high left elbows and cream teas. In a sense, it is simply taking *Test Match Special* to its 21st-century, online conclusion, involving the readers and waxing irrelevant when the fancy takes the commentator. It also owes a debt to the open-minded approach taken by Channel 4: don't feel embarrassed to explain the game's fundamentals to fans who used to regard cricket as slightly less accessible than the Holy Grail and you might be surprised by the response. But where *TMS* and Channel 4 (or, now that English cricket is more interested in cash than reaching the masses, Sky Sports) cannot compete with the OBO is in the workplace, where cricket's ability to indulge reality-avoiders comes into its own. Many is the time I have begun my pre-match musings a few minutes later than advertised and had my inbox deluged with angry readers demanding to know where the hell I had got to and didn't I realise they'd give their eye teeth for such a job and who did I think I was anyway, hmm? A day at the cricket is a day of glorious unreality, and the OBO is probably the next best thing if the day job is starting to get you down.

It also feels like a more democratic medium than the traditional outlets. Even *TMS*, famed for its appeal to the less hard-core cricket follower, has occasionally been coloured by old-fashioned thinking. When asked to explain the programme's enduring popularity by *Wisden Cricket Monthly* magazine in 2003, Henry Blofeld – the one who wears the bow tie and is an expert on buses and pigeons – explained: 'Over half the audience is female and they don't want technical cricket stuff. They want the sound of a comforting voice while they're doing the housework, or whatever they're doing.' Oh, just the housework I should think, Blowers. I hope I can say without sounding too smug that the OBO treats its female readers with a comforting voice minus the assumption of a mop and dishcloth.

Humorous, instant, online and equal-opportunity, the OBO seems to tick all the boxes demanded by contemporary cricket coverage. But it also ticks another: it is dirt cheap. The writer is not, as some readers seem to think, penning his indulgences under the Antiguan sun with a rum punch only a colonial snap of the fingers away, but is trying to block out the chatter of the sports desk while gagging on a polystyrene helping of watery tea and sitting in front of a malfunctioning TV. It is a form of reporting much loved by increasingly concerned accountants. And, partly for that reason, it is a form of reporting that will not replace newspaper journalism, which demands someone to be in the thick of things, and which – despite some of its excesses – continues to keep at bay the worries once aired by C.L.R. James. Writing in 1985, James felt that the

TV-driven cult of instant analysis was damaging cricket's natural inclination towards the reflective. 'You cannot analyse a five-day cricket match or five five-day matches in that way,' he warned. 'The result is that we have a series of front-page observations, dramatic moments, astonishing successes, astonishing failures – everything or nothing, governed by the remorseless claims of the television's audience waiting for the event which will summarise the day's play or the morning's play.'

It hasn't quite come to pass, even in the age of 24-hour news. But what would James have made of the OBO? Imagine if you were writing the commentary when a ghostly email dropped from the man himself. 'WICKET! Panesar b Johnson 0 (103 all out) Well, that's that – another Ashes series down the pan as Monty shoulders arms, loses his off-stump, and glances around at the prostrate pole which seems to symbolise so much of England's limpness in this series. Meanwhile, C.L.R. James has written in with some advice for Richard Baxter (44th over), who if you'll recall was trying to pluck up the courage to ask out Mandy in Advertising. "To establish his own identity, Caliban, after three centuries, must himself pioneer into regions Caesar never knew," points out CLR. "What do they know of Mandy who only Mandy know?" Richard, I think CLR is suggesting that Jessica in Accounts is the more viable option. Good luck!'

9

THE LANGUAGE

ANYONE WHO writes for a living – and most members of the press, when trapped in a half-nelson, would place themselves in that category – will remember their formative experiences and probably wince. A couple of my own spring to mind. Back in my university days, I was asked to write an essay about Goethe's *Faust*, which, with mis-leading simplicity, comes in two parts. The first is just about manageable with the aid of an English translation. The second requires a crack squad of Bletchley Park code-breakers and a doctorate-level knowledge of classical antiquity. It is, in short, a bugger. My tutor was an exacting, no-nonsense Scot with a moustache as clipped as his vowels and a barely disguised disdain for undergraduates who didn't know their Kantian Categorical Imperative from their elbow. Professor Nisbet's verdict on my effort? 'You still suffer from conceptual imprecision, lack of philo-sophical understanding and at times loose use of language.' Otherwise, an unadulterated triumph.

Three years later, I wrote my first article for *Wisden Cricket Monthly*, where I was spending a few weeks following graduation doing work experience to delay my entry into the real world. The article tried to analyse the struggles of county cricket's overseas stars, only to turn into the definitive 'hostage to fortune' – an assertion disproved between the time it is written and the time it is published – when Brian Lara thrashed 226 for Warwickshire against Middlesex shortly after. Then again, I could hardly complain, because what eventually appeared on the page bore little resemblance to my earnest and painstaking first draft. 'It's not bad,' said my editor, Tim de Lisle, gently clearing his throat for the inevitable 'but'. 'But it reads like an essay.' Tim proceeded to point out how the piece would not lose anything if I deleted that entire sentence and replaced it with a 'but'. Whole paragraphs were excised as I vowed never again to write the words 'notwithstanding', 'furthermore' and 'therefore' or to call Phil Simmons 'the burly Trinidadian all-rounder' or to accuse Mushtaq Ahmed – or anyone else, ever! – of 'flattering to deceive' or to use the word 'garner' ('great bowler, bad verb'). It was a massacre.

Like any aspiring professional cricketer, however, I learned my lessons and came away clutching the positives. And I like to think that without the advice from the Professor and Tim I might not have embarked on this strange career dabbling in the language of cricket. Like my tutor, cricket cannot stomach conceptual imprecision: after all, a leg-stump half-volley does not leave much room for philosophical misunderstanding. And, as with my initial *WCM* offering, cricket writing is at its least digestible when it is long-winded. There is usually so much to cram into a 500-word match report for the *Guardian* that brevity is not only a virtue but a necessity. Yet with these handy hints come problems of their own, at least for the newspaper journalist. County cricket reports in one or two of the broadsheets have become so condensed that pieces cede to set pieces: refuge is taken in cliché because cliché is safe, quick and simple. It saves space. Thus, a typical 180-word report on Hampshire v Warwickshire in, say, the *Daily Telegraph* might read like this:

Hampshire, having won the toss on a pitch that offered early assistance to the seamers, were yesterday inspired by a devastating spell from James Tomlinson, who achieved lavish movement in the air and off the seam to return career-best figures of seven for 34 as the visitors were bundled out for 132. It was Warwickshire's lowest score at the Rose Bowl, but their batsmen had only themselves to blame, and the umpires confirmed that the flurry of wickets had as much to do with poor technique against the swinging ball as any demons in the pitch. Ian Bell resisted manfully for a three-hour half-century after Warwickshire had lost their first three wickets with only 19 on the board, but when he was sixth out, disastrously padding up to Tomlinson's inducker, the rest followed like a pack of cards. Sean Ervine's diving catch at second slip to see off Darren Maddy was particularly memorable. Faced with 23 overs to see out before stumps, Hampshire reached 64 for the loss of Michael Brown, who poked James Anyon to Tony Frost before he had scored.

It's not especially inspiring, but if the writer had wasted some of his precious space describing the cloud formations or the expression on Anyon's face when the umpire turned down his umpteenth shout for lbw, he might have had the editor on the phone wondering why, precisely, he felt the sudden urge to turn into William Wordsworth. No, clichés are at times an inevitable part of cricket's language: assistance is always early, a spell devastating, movement lavish, resistance manful, and padding-up disastrous. Oh, and batsmen – golden rule, this, in the grimly all-knowing world of the county press-box – *always* have themselves to blame when they fail to counter the swinging ball.

The readers know it too. I once invited subscribers to my *Guardian* website column, 'the Spin', to email in with their favourite cricket clichés. I was curious to see if consensus could be reached about the worst crimes against the language. I was not disappointed. 'Any lbw shout that is not "absolutely plumb" has "done too much" and is "just drifting" down the leg-side,' wailed Andrew. 'Any leg-side shot played by a subcontinental player is "wristy", while good timing is either "superb" or "exquisite",' grumbled Thomas. 'When he hits it, it stays hit,' pointed out Yajnaseni. Wrote Peter: 'Shots in the air are "lofted" but if they get caught, why has the player "holed out"?' On it went. 'That one missed off-stump by a coat of varnish,' chuckled Roland. Will had a wish: 'Oh, to read two consecutive articles without Sir Frederick Flintoff being described as "talismanic" or, worse still, as "England's talisman",' he lamented. 'A "talisman" is a trinket thought to give protection against evil. You know, the sort of thing you pick up for 50p in Romford market on a Saturday afternoon.' For Richard, 'cricket was the winner'.

It's easy to laugh, but it is the kind of trap we all fall into. Sometimes clichés trip off the tongue before you even realise . . . you've. Used. Them. Why, for example, is dressing-room tension invariably described as 'internecine warfare', when the worst you are probably talking about is a row between the Derbyshire captain and his opening bowler about which end he wanted? Why is a not particularly large first-innings lead ('slender', naturally) always 'eked out', as if it is a beggar or freelance journalist trying to scrabble about for his next feed? Why are bespectacled cricketers referred to as 'studious' when the chances are they are simply short-sighted and having trouble with their contact lenses? Why do northern opening batsmen ('gritty' more often than not) tend to possess 'impenetrable' defences, when even the flimsiest of firearms would get through them? Why are Pakistani leg-spinners forever 'mysterious' when it is quite clear to everyone that Graeme Hick was done by the googly? Why are Australian openers 'uncompromising' when you would hardly expect them to ask an English seamer's permission to whack him back over his head for a one-bounce four? Why are New Zealand medium-pacers 'nagging' when they are hardly making the ball talk, let alone pester? Why are young fast bowlers 'raw' when the truth is they are just not very good? Perhaps the reason new additions to cricket's lexicon are lapped up with such enthusiasm is that every-one wants to use them before they become stale. Yet already the description of Kevin Pietersen's top-hand whip through midwicket off the front foot while his back leg kicks up behind him – first called the 'flamingo' by David Hopps of the *Guardian* – feels like an accepted part of cricket's verbal menagerie. All clichés were original once (he sighed).

It might not help that cricket-speak is not limited to the world of cricket, because there are few greater linguistic infractions than a cliché that becomes a cliché outside its natural habitat. While researching a piece for *Wisden* on the burst of cricket-related headlines that appeared in the non-sports sections of the national papers during the 2005 Ashes – yes, those sun-dappled days when cricket was the new football – I came across clichés so hideous that I was sick as a parrot. A prime example could be found in a headline on a piece about the Bank of England in the business pages of the *Independent*: 'On a sticky wicket, the Governor opts for the forward defensive.' That was just for starters. 'Mervyn King is stumped when it comes to the true state of the economy so for now he'll just keep playing each ball as it comes,' enthused the first line of the article. Never mind the fact that sticky wickets became a thing of the past when uncovered pitches went the way of the dodo in the early 1980s. Or that some batsmen's preferred method of batting on them was not to defend but to slog – in the belief that you might as well score runs before a ball came along with your name on it (oops, another cliché there . . .). Or that once Mervyn King had been stumped, the only balls he would have been playing would have been in his own mind. Or that it is impossible to play each ball in any other way than 'as it comes'. Never mind all that! No, what mattered was that the business pages of the *Independent* (the business desk of any newspaper is full of frustrated cricket writers) knew the words would resonate with readers who did not have the faintest idea of what a sticky wicket really was but who knew damn well they did not want to be caught on one. 'Have a good day, darling. And watch out for those sticky wickets!'

Cricket writers know it is not possible to use the sticky-wicket class of cliché in their copy because they would be a) laughed at by their peers and b) sacked. Years ago I wrote a piece for a friend who worked for the *Independent on Sunday* on, you guessed it, the business pages. The paper was running a series of articles about sporting events with a networking bent: Ascot, Cowes, the Walthamstow dog track, that sort of thing. My brief was to point out the potential business benefits of attending the Lord's Test and I filed a fairly straight article explaining where the social hobnobs were likely to hang out when they were not wasting their time actually watching the play. When I opened the paper a few days later, I was confronted with the following opening paragraph: 'The purists might splutter into their gin and tonics, but Test matches these days have corporate professionalism bowling unplayable googlies at quaint amateurism.' It was a cruel travesty of my original offering. I retched quietly, glanced around the *Wisden* offices where I was working a weekend shift and placed my copy of the paper at the bottom of my rucksack. The only thing that prevented my career being nipped in the bud there and then was the fact that the business pages of the *Independent on Sunday* are read by only a handful of diehards and none of them happened to be my editor. Had my words appeared in the *News of the World*, I would have been for the high jump.

Such is the lot of the suffering cricket writer. We nod patiently but scream inwardly when non-connoisseurs tell us how rude a googly is. We retire sweating and shaking to the bathroom when they titter at the idea of 'bowling a maiden over'. And we kick the cat under the table when they latch on to the erotic potential of being stroked through the covers. But let's face it: cricket as sexual innuendo can sometimes be too tempting to resist. During England's tour of West Indies in 2004, the *Sunday Mirror* published far-from-incriminating photos of David Gower in a bar . . . talking to a woman! To call the story a tabloid sting would be to dignify it with too much cunning: it was one of those grubbily misleading tales that is usually held over until August's silly season and which seems to have been commissioned with the clichés alone in mind. And sure enough, under an imaginative headline that bellowed 'HOWZAT!' the article began thus: 'This is the moment when England cricket legend David Gower made a tipsy bid to bowl a maiden over.' As cricket lovers groaned at the predictability of it all, the *Sunday Mirror* continued unabashed: 'But he was left at silly mid-off when the pretty brunette made a run for it.'

Things got sillier at the height of Ashes-mania in 2005. The Sunday tabloids ran gloriously hoary kiss-'n'-tells involving Kevin Pietersen and Simon Jones (with cricket/sex-speak to match), and a press release landed in my inbox from eCondoms, who called themselves 'the UK's largest mail-order company', not to mention 'the best online condoms shop for quality condoms'. With credentials like that, you would expect equally high-quality sales patter. Alas, no. 'With the Aussies boasting a line-up of superb bowlers,' read the email, 'picking the right balls is vital, so knowing your googly from your doosra has never been more important for both Michael Vaughan and the boys, and armchair fans alike.' Quite what picking the right balls had to do with contraception was not adequately explained. But, hey, the mere mention of a googly was sure to plant saucy thoughts in readers' minds. And, hang on, didn't doosra sound vaguely impolite if you thought about it hard enough, especially as bowlers seem to spend half their waking hours rubbing the ball suggestively up and down their crotch! All eCondoms needed to do was toss a couple of weird-sounding cricket words into the mix and allow our fertile imaginations to do the rest.

As cricket became sexier, so sex seemed to become more like cricket. In May 2006, the *News of the World* ran a double-page spread with pictures of Shane Warne in his underpants mucking around with two young ladies, one of them wielding a large blow-up appendage. The *Guardian* website's teatime football email, The Fiver, christened Warne the 'tabloid punchline', and here he was living down to expectations. 'Wicket ace Warne's leg over with 2 maidens (and a 4ft inflatable googly)' ran the headline, ignoring the fact that the inflatable was not a googly or even a goolie. The story began by horribly mixing its bowling and batting metaphors. 'Legendary bowler Shane Warne was on red-hot form the night he took two for dirty sex in a three-hour spell at the crease. And the randy Aussie cricket ace had model pals Emma Kearney and Coralie Eichholtz in a spin as he topped their figures again and again in a memorable innings at Emma's flat last Thursday.' We later hear all about the 'giant inflatable middle stump' and learn that Warne asked the 'wicked maidens' for 'more LB double-phew at the weekend'. In fact, the whole affair could not have been a more obvious set-up if the fake sheikh himself had appeared from under the bed asking Warne to repeat his name into a tape recorder. But for the right-thinking reader – i.e. the cricket-lover – that was far from the worst of the piece's offences. The *News of the World* has plumbed depths in its time, but its mangling of cricket's terminology must rank as some kind of nadir.

At moments like this, we can be forgiven for feeling strangely defensive about the language of cricket. And then we go and write po-facedly about rank long-hops and silky cover-drives as if we wouldn't touch a cliché with a bargepole. It was ever thus. Read a match report from the late 19th century and the best innings tend to be either 'capital', 'uncommonly good' or 'fine' (a word that unusually combines brevity with pomposity and, for some reason, is still used as a compliment on a regular basis by cricket commentators and wine buffs when the rest of the world regards it as the default answer to the question 'How are you?'). Leaf through early editions of *Wisden* and you can never quite get away from the image of a permanently tut-tutting great-uncle. 'The opening day's play was of a startling character,' begins the report on Leicestershire v Somerset in August 1893, steadying itself on the arms of its upholstered rocking chair. 'The crush at the gates on the first day was great and lasting beyond all precedent,' proclaims the account of the Eton–Harrow match at Lord's in 1872. What, so the queue was quite long? Elsewhere, the old journalistic notion of beginning in the middle of things is bowled neck and crop. Here's the start of *Wisden*'s report on the game between Yorkshire and Nottinghamshire in 1875. 'Pleasant cricketing weather favoured this match, wherein 274 overs were bowled for 360 runs from the bat, and nineteen of the thirty-four wickets down were bowled.' The result – a six-wicket win for Nottinghamshire, since you ask – makes a bashful appearance in the last sentence. Adjectives were in short supply; metaphors non-existent. The language of cricket reflected the austerity of the age. 'Cricket was associated with religion,' wrote the historian L.C.B. Seaman of Victorian England. 'Just as freemasons referred to God as the Great Architect of the Universe, young cricketers were taught to think of Him as the One Great Scorer, and almost to regard a Straight Bat as second in religious symbolism only to the cross of Jesus.'

Neville Cardus, the old *Manchester Guardian*'s music and cricket correspondent, changed all that. Sure, he made things up. Yes, the cricket he saw seemed to bear a striking resemblance to his state of mind on any given day. Absolutely, his imagery could be so painfully rich that he put the 'ow' into flowery. But it was a darn sight more entertaining than reading a sporting version of Hansard. Cardus was especially good on the Battle of the Roses between Lancashire and Yorkshire, where he often seemed more fascinated with imagined comments from the crowd than the actual cricket. Being a Lancastrian – Cardus was born in Rusholme, now the curry home of Manchester – he had particular fun with Yorkshiremen. In his account of the 1927 Roses match, in which Lancashire defeated the old enemy at Old Trafford for the first time in eight years, Cardus repeatedly places himself in the mind of the suffering Yorkshire followers. 'Oh, Emmott! What were t'a thinkin' of agean? Why didn't tha get out leg-before? Thee and thy fancy stroakes!' These days, a cricket writer may come up with the old 'wag in the crowd' line to work a good joke from a press-box colleague into his copy, but when he does so, it is with the tacit blessing of Cardus.

And where Cardus trod, others followed: Raymond Robertson-Glasgow, known as 'Crusoe' to his friends, Alan Ross, Matthew Engel, Peter Roebuck. Ross was almost as readable on peripherals like the weather as he was when applying his delicious similes to the game itself. When rain fell at The Oval in 1956, he had this to say: 'The crowd, like dolphins breaking surface, was soon getting to its feet, struggling into macintoshes and balancing paper hats. Within twenty minutes the players were off: and again there was the vilely familiar spectacle of covers being pushed on, the sky behind the Vauxhall cranes like a damp dishcloth and the atmosphere one of boredom, hope and endurance as inextricably entwined as the colours of the national flag.' Today's editors would be in touch straight away if anyone dared to file such luxuries. But it sure beats 'rain stopped play'. Cricket being cricket, this poetical strain forever runs parallel to the more high-minded and literal approach taken by the likes of Jim Swanton and John Woodcock, giants in their own right. For not everyone followed the Cardusian template. He was supposed to have been lost for words when Sid Barnes, the Australian Test batsman who later became a straight-talking, no-flourishes journalist, made him an offer during the 1950–51 Ashes: 'Look here, Neville. I've got an idea. What about me slipping a carbon paper into my copy today for you and you can do the same for me tomorrow. We both write the same sort of stuff.'

And what of today? Luscious prose is still valued, but perhaps it has given way, in newspapers at least, to the need to delve inside the players' minds. We have all become amateur psychologists, which might explain why the players increasingly shy away from baring their souls. As I've already discussed, clichés have become the default discourse, so much so that when Monty Panesar faced the press after taking four cheap West Indies wickets at Old Trafford in 2007, he entered the room to find a sheet of A4 on the table in front of him bearing the legend: 'REMEMBER TO SAY: GOOD AREAS, WORK HARD, KEEP IT SIMPLE'. One of the journalists had decided that poking fun was the best way to avoid another ten minutes of prepackaged verbiage. Monty sat down, saw the advice, started laughing and began to look round the room to spot the guilty party. What followed was like a game of Articulate, in which he tried to convey his favourite principle of keeping the ball in the right areas without using the actual words. 'You've just got to make sure you're getting the balls . . . in the areas you want to get them,' he said at one stage as previously somnolent hacks gripped the sides of their chairs to stop themselves laughing. 'You've got to let the wicket do what it's doing. It's important to get the balls where you want to get them.' Looking back, 'right areas' might have been preferable, although later in the summer Stuart Broad hinted at a nightmarish vision of the future for all journalists when he pointed out, in apparent seriousness, that 'areas is the way forward'. So ingrained had 'areas' become in the mind of the modern bowler that it now took a singular verb, as if it were a concept, like ethics. 'His areas is very good, but he needs to work on his sledging . . .'

Some in the dressing room go even further towards the language of gobbledegook. This strange tongue comes most naturally to coaches, who at times feel the need to justify their positions by dressing up simple pieces of advice as if they were gobbets of wisdom from Kahlil Gibran's *The Prophet*. No coach alive has gone a season without, for example, extolling the virtues of 'controlling the controllables', which basically means don't worry about the tornado that might strike Hove seconds before you are about to reach three figures. Duncan Fletcher was forever exhorting his players to 'come to the party' and 'put their hand up', when he could just as easily have asked them for runs and wickets. But the most fluent speaker of this tortured lingo was John Buchanan, the coach of the most successful Australian team in history. Buchanan's exact role in Australia's success was a moot point, and Shane Warne never tired of pointing out that he had always regarded a coach as the thing you get to the ground in (his assertion that Buchanan 'over-complicates issues' goes down as a rare example of Warne underegging the pudding). Possibly stung by the whispered suspicion that even a chimp could have coached an Australian team containing Steve Waugh, Ricky Ponting, Glenn McGrath and Warne himself, Buchanan would lapse into gobbledegook on a regular basis. After Australia's bowlers had sent down a string of costly no-balls against England at Edgbaston in 2005, for example, Buchanan insisted that he had encouraged them to 'implement self-management processes'. After a transcript of the press conference was sent to the EU for translation, it emerged that Buchanan had been pleading with his bowlers to bloody well keep part of your front foot behind the popping crease, mate. 'We didn't know what Buch was talking about a lot of the time,' said Waugh in 2006, 'so we were pretty happy for the papers to interpret it for us!' Which they did, mercilessly.

In one respect, cricket's increasing tendency towards gobbledegook mirrors the corporate speak of the outside world, so much so that some newspapers offer charts containing a group of set phrases for readers to tick off when they hear them used by TV commentators. To pluck an example from the *Guardian* on Twenty20 finals day in 2007: 'Charles Colvile introduces programme with "It's fast, it's furious, it's a high-octane festival of cricket – and it's live from Edgbaston only on Sky Sports!"'

In another respect, cricket revels in its tendency ot understate. Because, sexual gags aside, the game does euphemism like no other. Colin Milburn, the roly-poly

England batsman whose career was brought to a sadly premature end when he lost the use of his left eye in a car accident, was never fat, chubby, overweight, obese or just a plain porker. No, he was always 'well-built' – as if he had David Hasselhoff's six-pack rather than his own keg of ale. More recently, the former England chairman of selectors, David Graveney, referred to Rod Marsh's contributions in selection meetings as 'forthright', presumably in the way Marsh's contributions from behind the stumps when he kept wicket for Australia were forthright. Then there was Bishan Bedi's assessment of India in 2003. 'The concentration levels and the self-esteem of the current Indian side are seldom stable,' he said, presenting onlookers with plenty of opportunity to read gleefully between the lines.

Why the obfuscation? Perhaps because we are always shocked when cricket goes for the jugular. Bodyline appalled because of its directness and violence, particularly in the country on its receiving end. The West Indian quicks who ruled world cricket for a decade by giving the batsmen a couple of deliveries in their half of the pitch offended purists who felt cricket was a subtler game than that. The Indian Premier League was viewed as the Apocalypse. Slog is a dirty word, as if it is somehow more noble to disguise the fact that you are trying to score quick runs. Nothing is more revered in the game than the cover-drive that just beats the fielder to the boundary – timing, you see, rather than power – or high-quality leg-spin that, bit by bit, plays with the batsman's mind and unpicks his technique. Cricket admires unflashy values like guts and discipline, and feels a touch uncomfortable when Kevin Pietersen dyes his hair and pulls off the front foot. Euphemism is its lingua franca for a good reason.

Or perhaps I'm being very English about it all. Perhaps Lord Mancroft, once a Tory MP, had a point when he described cricket as a 'game which the English, not being a spiritual people, have invented in order to give themselves some conception of eternity'. And perhaps we get all twitchy when that conception is disturbed. The Australians, for example, have always talked with much more clarity about the sport, and possibly with a few more asterisks too. I once shared a beer on a tour of the sub-continent with an Australian coach, who was bemoaning the timidity of some of the batsmen in his team. 'They come to me and say, "[name deleted], what can I do? I'm scared of hitting the ball." And I just looked at them and thought, "Sheesh, I can't do bloody everything for them!"' Let's face it, Australia was always going to be the natural breeding ground for the World Series of a straight-talker like Kerry Packer, who introduced the idea of a camera at each end of the ground because no one 'wants to watch a batsman's bum for half the match'.

So it was bemusing to be there for the 2006–07 Ashes and find that a national debate had arisen about the rudeness or otherwise of the word 'Pom'. As a member of the great unwashed myself, I can assure any Australian readers that I have never so much as flinched at the epithet. Anyway, aren't nicknames supposed to be proof of affection? Steve Waugh regarded their usage by the Australian Ashes team in 2005 as a sign of weakness: 'I noticed them at the start of last summer using the England players' nicknames in the press and I thought, "We're in a bit of trouble here",' he told Nasser Hussain in a *Daily Mail* interview in 2006. Yet here we were, thanks to the visit of the England cricket team, debating whether to ban a word that could only offend the thin-skinned, the politically ultra-correct and those British expats who were sick and tired of being abused by Australians (in other words, all of them). At one stage a group called British People Against Racial Discrimination complained to the Advertising Standards Board in Australia about an advert for Tooheys beer that claimed it was 'cold enough to scare a Pom'. A BPARD spokesman was quoted as follows in an Australian newspaper: 'The Oxford Dictionary classes Pom as being derogatory just like wog, wop, dink, dago, coon and abo. It's every bit as bad as the term nigger.' The same spokesman went on to complain that Australian fans taunted British fans about 'your smell, your body odour, your bad breath, your buck teeth, your whingeing', while 'the worst you hear from the Barmy Army is that Aussies are sheep shaggers and you all live in a penal colony'.

The implication that your average Briton would rather be caught rogering Flossy than be accused of halitosis is curious enough. But not quite as curious as the idea that a cricket series was being used as the playing field for linguistic point-scoring. The matter became so serious that the Australian cricket board asked for a ruling from the Human Rights and Equal Opportunity Commission, who advised that use of the word 'Pom' in isolation was not in itself offensive, but that it would be if used in conjunction with a less polite tag. As Ben Fenton wrote in the *Daily Telegraph*: 'The last time an Englishman inside an Australian cricket ground was called a "Pom" without the addition of a hurtful, racist, offensive or humiliating epithet is lost in the mists of time.' So, Pommie bastard it was then. Since Prince Charles once recalled being called the very same during a two-term spell at Geelong

Grammar in Victoria in 1966, we are all in pretty decent company.

If the Aussies like to call a spade a bloody shovel, mate, what about that other great cricketing powerhouse, India? The answer is that it is not possible to say with any great certainty. One newspaper might call it a delightful digging implement; another might call it a magnificent garden friend. Because if there's one thing Indian papers do better than any nation in the world, it's high-octane hilarity. In a country of more than a billion people and – at times it seems – almost as many newspapers, the need to stand out can do weird and wonderful things to a writer. The day after I had been in Delhi to report on an England defeat in a one-day international, the *Times of India* ran a colour piece on the atmosphere at the stadium. The colour piece sits at the opposite end of the spectrum from the news piece: it is impressionistic, indulgent, reflective and might, if you're lucky, contain one or two gags. Facts, to invert the much-quoted maxim of C.P. Scott, are most definitely not sacred, while comment is well and truly free. Anyway, the *Times of India* piece kicked off like this: 'Attempting to pinpoint the mood at the Kotla [stadium] on 28/3 would be like trying to drive a thumbtack through a ray of golden sun.' As a means of elegantly telling the reader that words had failed you, it took some beating. Yet, among Indian newspapers, it was very much par for the course.

It's one thing for a reporter to put his or her own name to such musings, and which of us can say our prose hasn't veered into the realm marked 'purple' from time to time? But what really tickled me during that trip to India in early 2006 was the way in which the floridity carried over into ghosted columns, in which a journalist writes up a chat with a player under the player's name. Now I realise that by writing what I am about to write, I am going against the spirit of a piece of advice from Neville Cardus: 'It is wise not to be too rude about autobiographies; you never know who has written them.' And it is true that ghosting can be a notoriously tricky business: the journalist in question must make the column sufficiently juicy to please his editor and enlighten the public without making the player himself look like the very soul of indiscretion (and that's before his agent gets involved). But one of the golden rules is to try to stick as faithfully as possible to the voice of the player whose name, after all, appears above the words in the paper. So if you're ghosting Phil Tufnell, for example, steer clear of Shakespeare. And if you're ghosting Graham Gooch, well, try to bear in mind that he is known for being pretty direct, slightly downbeat and, if his ruthlessly efficient batting modus operandi is anything to go by, more interested in substance than style.

Yet here was Gooch every day in the Indian papers telling readers that England had collapsed 'like a ramshackle hut in a gale' and that 'it is difficult to avoid being repetitive for England yet again walked the same filthy path and met the same wretched fate'. (In other words, the idiots lost again.) Now read aloud this next section, in which 'Gooch' touches on Rahul Dravid's press-conference manner, in the great man's high-pitched Essex tones: 'I have evinced a keen interest in Dravid's public stance on issues and men. Most of the time he hams or is being repetitive. He defends his men and opposition, and there is never a harsh word for a pitch or a curator. He is nearly always politically correct and nearly always boring.'

Or how about 'Gooch's' analysis of Virender Sehwag's struggles outside off-stump? 'His initial bravado has given way to scepticism. Sehwag in repose at the crease has resembled a cat ready to pounce on anything which comes his way. A cobra in coil, a panther on haunches, a falcon in that strategic patrolling of the sky.' The thought of Gooch rousing his players when he was Essex and England captain with a wistful look towards the heavens and an exhortation to be a falcon in that strategic patrolling of the sky is too magnificent for words. Yet these are the words his ghost, presumably determined to avoid the charge of being boring, placed in his mouth.

Still, at least we knew roughly what Goochie was trying to say. It was a roundabout kind of clarity, which is preferable to not having the foggiest. How about the man from Chicago who sounded like he was the official cheerleader of a West Indies cricketer but turned out to be a journalist for the *Morton Grove Champion*? His attempts to explain the laws of cricket to the inhabitants of the Windy City culminated in this gem: 'Runs can be scored in several ways, like when a ball touches the ground and then leaves the playing area, or when the pair of batters (there are two on the field) run up the base line and switch places before an out can occur.' I promise this is not a cheap excuse to poke fun at the Americans. After all, they were playing international cricket twenty-four years before England and Australia got their act together. (It's true.) But it does show that the language of cricket can leave you badly exposed if you don't do your homework.

A friend got in touch once to tell me that his fiancée, an Anglo-Japanese woman who knew even less about the game than the readers of the *Morton Grove Champion*, was on her way to Lord's to spend the day in a corporate box watching a one-day international between England and India. She was feeling less than riveted at the prospect and had been teased in advance by her mainly male colleagues about her lack of cricketing nous. Concerned, my friend wondered whether I could supply her with a string of informed one-liners that she could memorise and pluck out of thin air at appropriate moments. 'Only too happy to oblige,' I said. A few days later, my friend rang back to report that the day had been a triumph. After sitting quietly for the first hour or so, she had reduced her persecutors to stunned silence by observing quite loudly that 'I've never thought of Anil Kumble as a leg-spinner, really. More of a medium-pace purveyor of toppies.' As previously cocky city boys nervously loosened their ties and shifted on their seats, she added: 'Not to worry, though. Trescothick can be murderous with the slog-sweep.' By the time she had reeled off a dozen or so *bons mots*, she had achieved a new level of respect. Of all my dabblings in the language of cricket, this remains the proudest.

10

THE FUTURE

THE LANGUAGE of cricket and much more besides changed for good on 20 February 2008, the day WG, the Don and Bodyline were joined in cricket's lexicon by Reliance Industries Limited, GMR Holdings and, the biggest name in Bollywood, Shah Rukh Khan. Welcome to the Indian Premier League – or possibly 'IPL ki duniya mein swaagat hai'. It is a world in which the game's stars are divided into eight franchises ('teams' is so 20th century: wait for the references to 'our excellent franchise spirit') according to the bidding whims of the sub-continent's rich, famous and egotistical – a savage twist on the old school-playground scene of small boys lining up against a wall, hoping and praying not to be chosen last for the lunchtime kickabout. And, as the players suddenly set aside concerns about burnout in the knowledge that they were about to earn as much in six weeks as they generally did in a year, it was tempting to think back to Kerry Packer's cheery rejoinder to the Australian Cricket Board in 1976. 'Come on now, we're all harlots,' he said in an attempt to poach the TV rights. 'Name your price.'

Numbers so dizzying swirled around the lobby of Mumbai's Hilton Towers hotel, scene of this unprecedented auction, that even Packer might have rubbed his eyes in disbelief. Eight companies and celebrities had already paid well over US $700m between them for the honour of owning the franchises; they were about to lavish more than $40m on players' wages. India's one-day captain Mahendra Singh Dhoni was deemed worthy of a pay packet of $1.5m to play in a tournament that lasted forty-four days. Ishant Sharma, a 19-year-old fast bowler with five Tests behind him, picked up $900,000, which, we kept being told as if it added to the romance, wasn't bad for the humble son of an air-conditioning salesman. And Andrew Symonds went for $1.35m, thus becoming the best-paid pantomime villain in cricket history: without his childish run-ins with Harbhajan Singh over the preceding months, his attractiveness to the Indian market would have been questionable.

Elsewhere, the sound of pen on chequebook was scarcely less frantic. Sony Television and World Sport Group teamed up to fork out over $1bn to broadcast and promote the IPL for a decade, while a company called DLF Universal, an Indian real-estate developer, paid $50m to slap their name on the competition for five years. Neil Maxwell, an agent and also the CEO of the Kings XI Punjab franchise, working on behalf of the Australian IPL players, declared with some pride that wages were 'in the realms of the English Premier League, which for a long time players have wanted to aspire to'. Gosh, so that was why they were playing the game! Yes, the BCCI- and ICC-endorsed DLF IPL was more than a mouthful of capital letters. It was, so we were reminded repeatedly, the future itself. And you could either hop on for the ride or watch the gravy train purr off into the sunset. As I detailed my concerns in my column – to sum up: more cash equals less passion – I felt as idealistic as the student who stood in front of the tank in Tiananmen Square. 'Get back to your world of three men and a dog,' wrote one Indian reader, who obviously knew more about Grace Road on a wet Wednesday than he was letting on.

The sums of money involved were matched only by the speculation. Would the ICC, ever eager not to upset the all-powerful Indian cricket board, agree to an annual six-week window in which the IPL could showcase its wares without pesky distractions, such as Test cricket? And would the Test game increasingly resemble the uncle in the cardigan looking on from the corner of the pub as wild young Twenty20-somethings danced on the bar? Would the county championship, with its shires, outgrounds and ice-cream stalls, be affected? And would Ricky Ponting recover from his valuation of $400,000, a full $225,000 less than the price fetched by his uncapped compatriot David Hussey?

But behind the razzmatazz and the dollar signs lay the fundamental truth about cricket in 2008: it is, as someone once said, an Indian game invented by the British. Or, as Lalit Modi, the commissioner of the IPL and quite possibly the most powerful man in the game today, put it: 'India has been subservient for 100 years. People are used to dictating terms to us. We're just evening the playing field. And if it's our turn to have some glory, so much the better.'

Perceptions were changing quickly. Almost a year before the game's great players expressed their excitement about representing the Delhi Daredevils and the Chennai Super Kings, I had headed for the ECB's National Academy in Loughborough to interview Allan Donald. Given that he is a South African, Donald had been a strangely influential figure in my relationship with cricket over the years. He had helped cement in my mind at an impressionable age the idea that Dermot Reeve was one stump short of the full set (Reeve once swept him during a World Cup game). Yes, that's Allan Donald, the man who bowled so fast that his nickname, White Lightning, erred on the side of caution. He had been kept at bay by Mike Atherton during that glorious rearguard at Johannesburg, an innings which would forever encourage Englishmen to believe that the next great escape was just round the corner. A couple of years later, he single-handedly sparked a brief interest in the game in a former girlfriend of mine by getting all hot and bothered with Atherton at Trent Bridge. (It was an interest that did not last beyond the first day of the next Test, at Headingley, where the excitement of a pair of tickets soon gave way to England's joyless crawl to 230 all out.) And he reduced England to two for four on the opening day of the 1999 series at Jo'burg – one of those mornings where it seemed God was taking revenge for Britain's crimes in the colonies. He was, in short, a legend. And it turned out he was a very good talker too, especially for an Afrikaner who had arrived in England with a vocabulary presumably limited to 'howzat'.

Conversation turned to India. Three days earlier, the Indians had been lucky to escape from the first Test at Lord's with a draw. Steve Bucknor had failed to give their last man Sreesanth out to Monty Panesar, despite the fact he was hit just above the ankle in front of middle stump, at which point the light closed in and it began to rain. ('Rain saves [insert name of England's opposition]', when it had in fact done nothing of the sort, was the kind of gallows humour that had served England fans faithfully over the years. Now it really was true.) The second Test began in Nottingham the day after the interview and Donald, at the time the coach of England's fast bowlers, was still brooding over Lord's. To see him dressed in his shiny England tracksuit, bemoaning the bad luck of a team who once held on nine wickets down for a draw against his own South

African side, was to struggle with the surrealism of it all. It was as if Sachin Tendulkar had walked into the room screaming 'Pakistan! Zindabad!' or Brendon McCullum broken out into a lusty chorus of 'Advance Australia Fair'. Yet the passion for his new job was undoubtedly there, even if he left it soon after for a position with his former county, Warwickshire. We talked about his fourth Test appearance, against India at Port Elizabeth, a game in which he took twelve wickets and which thus became the moment he Announced Himself To The World, a rite of passage for any future international-class cricketer.

After Announcing Himself To The World, he moved swiftly on to the next tite of passage: Telling It The Way He Sees It. 'I got crucified by the South African Cricket Board for saying in a press conference that I thought India were gutless,' he said, fixing me in the eye as if I had just gloved him to the keeper and refused to walk. 'And I still believe they were gutless.' It did not seem like the moment to argue. This was a man who had made the Waugh twins look stupid – and they had been in possession of chunky bats and plenty of protective clothing. I was armed with a Dictaphone and a three-by-five-inch notepad. Still, journalistic fearlessness being what it is, I chanced my arm and wondered whether he had noticed the same gutless-ness among the 2007 Indians. I fully expected him to do something he rarely did during his career, and send down a tepid half-volley. Not a bit of it. 'I've seen the same frailties, definitely,' he said. 'India have always had certain individuals that have bailed them out, like a Tendulkar, or an Azharuddin or a Rahul Dravid. You just need to target them.'

You can guess what happened next. England targeted

them so well that India won the second Test at Trent Bridge at a canter, scoring almost 500 in conditions ideal for swing bowling. They then made 664 at The Oval to secure their first series win in England since 1986. Soon after that, they won the World Twenty20 competition in South Africa, a result which would convince a previously sceptical Indian public that this was a form of the game worth bothering about. And then they pushed Australia hard in a Test series down under, before walking off with the one-day Commonwealth Bank Trophy. But Donald's perspective, reasonable enough at the time, summed up the weird dichotomy that accompanies India everywhere they go. Off the field, they are cricket's superpower, generating between two-thirds and three-quarters of the sport's global revenue with their astronomical TV deals. On the field, they are perceived as often brilliant but occasionally vulnerable and unquestionably pampered, more than happy to duff up visiting teams on the brown, brown grass of home, but supine the moment they pass through the duty-free section at Mumbai airport. That win at Trent Bridge was only their fifth in England since 1932. But times are changing and by the late 2000s India finally seem poised to replicate their financial muscle with a bit of on-field flexing too.

It's not as if the raw materials aren't there. For someone, like me, who has emerged from a bus in Guwahati to be greeted by crowds like a Bollywood celebrity, it is odd to think that cricket in India needed a shock win over West Indies in the 1983 World Cup final to ensure its place in the people's affections. In 1980, India won its eighth and most recent Olympic gold medal in hockey. But thanks to complacency on the part of Viv Richards and Co at Lord's three years later, the focus shifted to cricket. Hockey never got another look-in. Cricket, on the other hand, seeps into every nook and cranny, from the bars to the backstreets, from chatting with taxi drivers to watching on television. If you are heading out to India, brush up on the latest scores. Cricket lubricates their conversation like beer does ours. Even a fleeting knowledge of Sachin Tendulkar's career stats can go a long way. I was in the country for April Fool's day in 2006, which seemed appropriate given the comedy show England were putting on for the one-day series at the time, when several newspapers plumped for the same gag: an old picture of a grinning Sourav Ganguly, the deposed captain, and a grinning Greg Chappell, the coach who had deposed him. 'Ganguly back in the Indian side' was the gist of the headlines. It was a decent stunt, but the idea of, say, the *Sun* leading its back page with the spoof news that Mark Ramprakash was planning to use a series of dance routines to assist the England batsmen with their footwork would be unthinkable; some sick crack about the footballer who refused a pay rise, maybe. But cricket? Many in England regard the sport as a joke, but not an April Fool's one.

When it comes to cricket in India, nothing surprises. Earlier in that tour, the England party had been in Nagpur, the largest city in central India, where the local Sunday paper, the *Hitavada*, included fifteen cricket articles among its sixteen pages. One of them was breathlessly headlined: 'Chappell acknowledged receipt of email,' which sounds like a bad joke in *Private Eye*. On the front page, the three main stories went like this: 'England Cook up a defiant story' (Alastair Cook had marked his Test debut with a century); 'Keep restraint, Pawar tells Chappell in surprise meet' (cricket politics in India demands as much coverage as the real thing); and, at the bottom, some inconsequential titbit about President Bush and a nuclear deal with Pakistan. But by giving its readers what they wanted, the *Hitavada* was merely doing its job. And so it went on. When England landed in nearby Indore for the last game of that tour, the local evening paper exclusively revealed that 'Andrew Flintoff was spotted visiting the mall today afternoon along with two of the doctors who have arrived with the team. While the player went around the mall guarded by six to seven police personnel, one of the doctors purchased two jeans from Sajan-Sajani.' And, with readers still reeling from the excitement, the report continued: 'Also the physiotherapist of English team [the use and abuse of definite articles in Indian English is one of its most characteristic quirks] enjoyed squash game and lunch at Hotel Sayaji. Nigel, Mike and Darren of the team management were seen at Sayaji poolside before having lunch.' The absence of a Mike or a Darren in the tour party was neither here nor there: what mattered was the vague presence of these mythical creatures, a story which is thought to have just squeezed out 'England player breaks wind' at the last minute.

At one stage a group of English journalists must have come perilously close to making the news themselves. Dining at Pizza Hut in the same mall in which Flintoff and the jeans-buying doctors caused such a rumpus, we were seated next to a large window which looked out onto the mass of shoppers. Every so often, a group of boys would stop, stare, point and then make a small gesture with their wrists: no, not the one you see at football grounds when the away team scores in front of the home fans, but the one a captain makes in the direction of the dressing room after the toss to indicate that his side are batting. Unlike most things that occur on India's roads, this signal was unambiguous. It asked: are you the England team? Even the most vigorous shake of the head was futile, and before we could as much as swallow a chunk of Cheese Fantastico to mouth 'no', tens of inquisitive faces were pressed à la Tiny Tim against the window to watch the 'England team' enjoy their meals. It seemed easier just to play along.

So much for the pizza: the biscuit was well and truly taken by the *Hindustan Times*'s coverage of England's one-day game at Jamshedpur. One article dug deep into its investigative resources to discover the menu for the two teams on the following day's chartered flight out of town ('pullao, mix vegetable, salad, bread roll, pickles, rajbhog limewater, fruit juices, cold drink and butter', since you ask). It went on to wonder whether the local hotel had come up with any special delicacies for the Indian wicket-keeper, Mahendra Singh Dhoni, who hails from nearby Ranchi. Indirectly quoting the director of the Yuvraj Palace hotel, the article declared: '[Mr] Chopra said the final menu would be confirmed only by Wednesday night. But sadly, the chances of serving local cuisine were very meagre.' Dhoni's disappointment was not recorded, but his mood might have lightened at the sight of another piece – 'British media goes gaga' – in which three English journalists were surprised to find themselves waxing lyrical about his brilliance. It was not that the journalists – including the *Daily Mirror*'s 'Michael Watkins', a man known to family and friends as Mike Walters – didn't rate Dhoni. Far from it. What struck them was that not one of them recalled ever being asked for a quote in the first place. In Britain, they make up quotes from the 'pals' of

A-list celebs, or 'onlookers' who just happen to speak the tongue of the tabloids. In India, they make up quotes from foreign cricket journalists, and everyone is happy.

But the surest sign of that trip that cricket had long ago moved from the realms of a cult to an all-out religion was a front-page item declaring that India's only defeat in the seven-match one-day series was all down to the 'vaastu'. Broadly speaking, vaastu is the Hindu equivalent of feng shui, and it was of course the only possible explanation for India's poor record at Jamshedpur's Keenan stadium. The article quoted one 'vaastu consultant' as saying that the venue 'still has problems with the dressing room'. With furrowed brow, he went on: 'The dressing room is considered as business area, and in vaastu, a flourishing business centre should be located in the North-West direction with its entrance towards the North.' The message was unambiguous. If Australian newspapers relegate rare defeats by England to the inside pages, then their Indian counterparts move them to the front but blame them on cosmic energy. (England could hardly complain: the former chairman of selectors Ted Dexter once blamed another loss on the alignment of the planets.) It was no wonder Andrew Flintoff's men looked fed up.

Yes, it's easy to poke fun, especially when a local Indian paper loses all sense of proportion. But, as with the inhabitants of Guwahati, you can understand why they might do it: England's visit to Jamshedpur was only the tenth day of international cricket there since it first hosted West Indies in 1983, and England had only visited once before, a time so long ago that the winning partnership was compiled by Neil Fairbrother and Dermot Reeve. No country spreads its matches more thinly. In all, over 40 venues have staged one kind of international cricket or another in India; next comes England with 23, of which only eight Tests, followed by Pakistan with 20. The upshot is that matches even in the large Indian cities are major events; in the rural outposts, they can feel as rare as an admission of guilt from Harbhajan Singh. Even so, it is hard to convey the sheer scale of the obsession without a degree of wry detachment. What other way is possible?

India's love of cricket is often equated with the English mania for football, and references to the English Premier League have peppered the IPL debate. But since India is home to over a billion people and England to 50 million, this is misleading by a factor of roughly 20. And all-engulfing though the Premier League might be, it has not mugged cricket in the same way as cricket has mugged everything else in India since Mohinder Amarnath and Madan Lal's big day out in 1983. Indeed, cricket in India has gone beyond mugging. It has entered the realms of kidnapping so ruthlessly that the hostages began sympathising with their abductors long ago. Cricket in India is Stockholm Syndrome on an unimaginable scale – and we're not just talking about overblown newspaper articles here. Writing in early 2006 on a blog called 'The Love of Cricket', Rajdeep Sardesai, the editor-in-chief of CNN-IBN (India Broadcast News), explained: 'We cover the cricket, but barely pay attention to the crisis engulfing other Indian sport. Knocked out of the Davis Cup by Korea, languishing in hockey and football, do we really care? It's no longer enough to blame these sports for failing to do enough to "market" themselves, or not throwing up stars. The fact is that these sports are caught in a vicious cycle of anonymity today, and we in the news media are contributors to the exclusion of certain sports from the public consciousness. I plead guilty.' Rather like global warming, everyone can see what is happening. It's just that no one has the inclination to do anything about it. When the Indian cricket board brokered a TV deal worth £350m over four years a month after Sardesai's lament, hockey and the glory days of the 1950 Olympics were the last things on anyone's mind.

The adoration of cricket in India is a source of constant fascination, especially for phlegmatic Englishmen who regard public displays of excitement as a damned poor show, quite frankly. Compare and contrast, for example, the reactions of the two nations when the TV camera pans across the crowd and settles on a group of spectators, one or two of whom just happen to be female. In England, it usually takes the fans a few seconds to realise they are live on television, at which point one will nudge another and point excitedly, but never ostentatiously, towards the big screen. By the time the nudgee has realised what is going on, it is too late and the cameraman has found another cleavage to peer down. In India, the fans seem to have an inbuilt mechanism for working out when the camera is pointing in their direction, like the Herdwick sheep who can be let loose in a Lake District field safe in the knowledge they will not stray beyond their traditional patch. And when that happens, they – the Indian fans, not the Herdwick sheep – go wild. If a gunman were to emerge on the pitch behind them and mow down the entire Indian team, these fans would be too busy dancing and waving to notice.

This particular brand of enthusiasm is alien to cricket

watchers in the western nations. In England, enthusiasm takes the form of Barmy Army black humour, although it can lapse too easily into unattractive triumphalism. In Australia, it can be found in the genuine belief that no other side on earth is fit to crack open their boys' tinnies. But in India, it is naive, ingenuous and captivating. And it is one of the reasons why their former coach John Wright wrote: 'When I finish with cricket in a professional capacity and get back to watching it purely for pleasure, I won't bother going to Lord's; I'll go back to India.'

India can do things to a man which the man might never have thought possible. One of my favourite mid-over ads on Indian TV during England's one-day series there in 2006 contained a sight that would never be allowed on British screens. Not only were Michael Vaughan and Andrew Flintoff standing in adjacent shower cubicles – they were singing to each other too. It was the kind of scene that risked a whole season's worth of piss-taking in your average county dressing room. The joke in the advert was that Flintoff kept coming out with the wrong words – we won't even go near the melody – as an increasingly impatient Vaughan kept correcting him. 'No!' he would say as if fighting back tears of frustration. 'It's ulalalalaleeeyo!' One Indian journalist assured me these were the sounds of an African mating song, so quite why Flintoff struggled to get his tongue round them was anyone's guess. And the product they were advertising? Kingfisher lager, of course. Yet here I am still talking about it.

Then there was the strange case of the guitar-strumming, vocals-loving Australian fast bowler who composed a ditty in half an hour during the Champions Trophy in India in 2006 and watched it rise to No. 2 in the

Indian charts. Brett Lee is better known for terrorising opening batsmen, but when he teamed up with Asha Bhosle, one of Bollywood's best-known singers, to inflict upon the world lyrics such as 'Can you tell a girl you don't know that you're the one for me?/Do you walk right up or play it cool or simply let her be?' he struck an unlikely chord with a cricket-mad nation. Interviewed about his foray into the Indian music industry at the Allan Border Medal evening in 2007, he could barely speak for the sound of mocking laughter. 'I've copped a fair bit of ribbing from the boys,' he smiled, as Andrew Symonds, a man who would rather be seen walking the streets of Melbourne in a pair of Union Jack boxer shorts than sing in public, roared with hilarity in the background. 'I've always wanted to do a song in India,' said Lee, as if it were as natural a career move as stepping into Glenn McGrath's shoes and taking the new ball for Australia. Still they laughed. But why exactly? To succeed commercially in India is to look forward to a long and prosperous retirement. Lee weighed up the amount of flak he would get and decided a raised profile in the land owning most of cricket's money was worth being called a flamin' sheila.

He is hardly alone. In late 2007, the breakaway Indian Cricket League staged its inaugural Twenty20 competition in the northern city of Panchkula, Chandigarh. The tournament was born after a Packer-style piece of entrepreneurialism by Zee Telefilms, India's largest media group, who had become increasingly fed up at their failure to secure the rights to broadcast the national team's matches. Packer responded to what he regarded as the intransigence of the Australian board by paying the world's best players big bucks to take part in World Series Cricket.

Zee, fronted by the former Indian all-rounder Kapil Dev, persuaded a few mainly ageing internationals to join mainly up-and-coming Indian youngsters under the banner of teams such as Mumbai Champs, Delhi Jets and Kolkata Tigers. The tournament was won by Chennai Superstars, which included players from Australia (Stuart Law and Ian Harvey), England (Chris Read), Sri Lanka (Russel Arnold) and Pakistan (Shabbir Ahmed). Chandigarh Lions, the beaten finalists, could boast a trio of Kiwis (Chris Cairns, Hamish Marshall and Daryl Tuffey) and South Africa's Andrew Hall. The Indian board retaliated by setting up the IPL with the official approval of the ICC to help put the rebel ICL in its place. Everyone joined in bar the English, who were too busy fretting over a Test series in New Zealand. The competion made Lee's musical adventure look like a prescient piece of business.

How times have changed. Between the 1992–93 tour of India and the visits in 2000–01 to Pakistan and Sri Lanka, England did not take part in a single bilateral series on the subcontinent. Not one. Any western visitor will know that an inordinate amount of time in any of those countries can be spent either visiting the toilet or hallucinating feverishly in bed. But the odd bout of diarrhoea or a night spent worrying you are Arjuna Ranatunga are hardly good enough reasons for depriving an entire generation of English cricketers of a vital chunk of their education. No, one of the biggest problems – and I use the word advisedly – faced by the English tourist on the subcontinent is, apparently, boredom. As I mentioned earlier, before England flew to Pakistan in 2005–06, the party line was that it was the kind of tour that brings the boys together because they spend so much time bonding –

or possibly bored witless – in their hotel rooms. Darren
Gough was not part of the touring group, but his advice
was particularly revealing. 'The boys will be playing their
computer games and watching DVDs,' he said. 'And if they
go to the High Commission then they'll find a bar there.
It's a lot of fun and the team will get even closer as a unit.
There are a lot of games provided. Things like Question of
Sport on a video conference and horse-racing games. It's a
great laugh. The horse-racing game is particularly good
fun, because there's a bookie involved.' Booze and
gambling, both banned in the real Pakistan beyond the
cloistered gates of the High Commission, would keep
England sane.

Yet by the end of a trip in which England lost the Tests
and the one-dayers, the joys of closeness had transmuted
into the claustrophobia of cabin fever. 'I don't like to
criticise anyone,' said the Pakistan fast bowler Shoaib
Akhtar as he cleared his throat to criticise someone, 'but
they seem to be going through the motions and not
enjoying the tour. Every part of the world is different and
if you are expecting the same in this country as back home
you might not get it.' That was a polite way of putting it,
and recalled the complaint made by the Pakistani umpire
Sajjad Asghar after Andy Caddick said 'things about my
country' during a tour match at Peshawar in November
2000. As this was England's first trip to Pakistan for 13
years, Caddick's outburst was not the height of tact.
Writing on his *Cricinfo* blog towards the end of the cabin-
fever tour of 2005–06, Kamran Abbasi – an Anglo-Pakistani
– wondered whether Pakistan might retaliate with spurious
fevers of their own when they visited England the following
summer. 'Disco fever might be one,' he wrote, 'particularly

likely to strike down fast bowlers who fancy themselves as party animals. Secularism fever might be another, a worrying condition that afflicts Muslims spooked by 24-hour licensing laws, low-cut dresses, and bacon butties. Or how about crap-weather fever, an intense allergy to the miserable climate of an English summer. The possibilities are endless.' The thing is, most top-class hotels in Pakistan and India are as good as, if not better than, their English counterparts. You couldn't wish for more luxurious surroundings in which to complain about the fact that you are being paid to travel the world and represent your country.

For some reason, the feeling persists that not all visiting cricketers make the most of their opportunities in the subcontinent. It was Phil Tufnell who notoriously told a journalist on England's farcical tour of India in 1992–93 that he had 'done the elephants, done the poverty, now can we go home?' Even taking into account the fact that, for a variety of reasons, Tuffers was never the best of travellers, the chapter in his autobiography covering the tour ('Done India') reads like the definitive manual of Anglo-Saxon insularity. At one point he sums up the process of getting from A to B in India like this: 'The usual scares in the air, including the occasion where the hydraulics failed as the plane was landing in Bangalore and the boys got out to see a hole the size of a coffin in the fuselage, and a game of hunt the rat on one train from God-knows-where to God-knows-where-else.' He ends the chapter by summing up the brief trip to Sri Lanka that was tagged onto the Indian leg: 'Bloody hot. Bloody lost. Done the poverty, done the elephants, done the mosquitoes, done the tantrum, done in. *Now* can I go home?'

Hammed up for comic effect though his views may have been, Tufnell was not alone in his suspicion of India. Ted Dexter reacted to England's mauling in the first Test at Calcutta by saying he would commission a report into the effects of smog on the English cricketers. Like so many English cricket inquiries, the results of this one have never been published – if indeed the inquiry was ever held in the first place – but since England lost that game by a mere eight wickets and the remaining two, at Madras (now Chennai) and Bombay (now Mumbai), by an innings, the only conclusion was that it had bugger all to do with the smog. In the end, it probably comes down to a fear of the unknown. One famous England player, landing in India for the first time, was supposedly greeted by a local cricket nut so awestruck to be in his presence that he fell to his knees and grasped his legs as if they belonged to Ganesh himself. Used to being pestered back home by nothing more than a handful of middle-aged groupies and a smattering of bespectacled men in anoraks brandishing the latest edition of *The Cricketers' Who's Who*, the player panicked and unleashed a swift uppercut.

Suspicion, of course, can be a two-way process. It's just that it is laden with historical baggage when exercised by the traditionally white cricket nations. My attempts to write about Indian cricket are occasionally met by cries of racism on the blog section of the *Guardian* website, never more so than when I accused the Indian board of 'grandstanding' over the Harbhajan Singh/Andrew Symonds spat at Sydney in January 2008. India briefly threatened to pull out of the tour after Harbhajan was banned for three Tests by the match referee Mike Procter for supposedly calling Symonds a monkey. And although the ban was later overturned by an independent inquiry because of a lack of evidence, it seemed to me – and plenty of other cricket writers, not a few of them Indian – that the Board of Control for Cricket in India knew they could throw their political weight around and get away with it. The comments section underneath my blog seethed with its usual mass of sporadic reason and rampant nationalism. 'The author is dreaming of the good old days of biased English ownership of the game,' insisted one blogger, who ended up sounding like George W. Bush on one of his less thoughtful days. 'The Asian line is clear: with us or against us! We don't believe in compromises.' Another blogger danced to a familiar tune: 'The comments look like lecturing how the Indians should behave.' A third was just plain outraged: 'This is disgusting, one-sided, racist writing at its worst. Reminds me of England of the 1960s . . . Do us all a favour, *Guardian,* and find this guy a job at the *Daily Mail.*' And so, tediously, on and so forth, et cetera, zzzzz . . . Look hard enough for offence and you will find it.

It is surely no coincidence that the most successful England captains in India have been those who have embraced the differences. On the 1976–77 tour, Tony Greig understood instinctively that the best way to win over the Indian crowds was to pander to their love of the visual and the melodramatic. Who needed Bollywood when you had Greig collapsing to the ground during the first Test at Delhi when a firecracker went off in the stands? After that, all he needed to do was bow theatrically to the spectators when he was fielding on the boundary and they were in the palm of his hands. England won 3–1. In *Yakking Around the World,* Simon Hughes was reminded of India's penchant for slapstick when he was visiting the country at the same time as Graham Gooch's band of miseries in 1992–93. Invited to a wedding in Mangalore on India's south-west coast, he was asked at very short notice to deliver a speech to '1,000 Indians, virtually all of whom are either noisily refilling their plates or chewing on marinated lamb shanks'. Hughes ransacked his treasure chest of cricket anecdotes for inspiration, but drew blanks with three quite serviceable gags. (Example: why do Pakistan bowlers win so many lbw appeals at home? Because when they appeal, they shout 'Where's Allah?', at which point the umpire sticks his finger towards the heavens.) Anyway, Hughes's saving grace, the story that eventually brought the house down, involved a childhood game of cricket with the groom in which the ball ended up on the roof of a block of flats. 'We were just going to get it,' he told his audience, 'when his dad appeared in the doorway angrily waving his umbrella.' The reaction? 'Uproarious laughter. It didn't die down for some time, after which I left the podium to hysterical cheering.' Hughes, far more open-minded and curious than the average cricketer, concluded that England's attitude that winter was not what it might have been. 'Smile and shrug' was his mantra for coping with the oddities the subcontinent can throw your way. 'England just whined and whinged.' Many years later, the New Zealand batsman Lou Vincent – not renowned as the sharpest stump in the kitbag – expressed the incredulity of a generation of western cricketers: 'I don't know how you Indians live here.'

It's true that the image of Indian cricket many westerners rely on is that of the burned effigy – a symbol of irrational devotion to a game that can switch from idolatry to hatred as easily as the flick of a coin. In fact, this image is as one-eyed a perspective as that of the effigy-burners themselves, especially as it is hard to fathom how cameramen always happen to be on the scene to record the latest inferno following an Indian defeat. For every effigy-burner there are far more standing by with a bucket of water. I know plenty of Indians who, like Inzamam-ul-Haq's team-mates in the lunch queue, wince at the excesses of their countrymen. And they are the main reason why the idea of India ruling the cricket world is not as ridiculous as it once seemed. This is a nation with an acute sense of its own pulling power. John Wright recalls meeting the Indian squad after a ten-day break and asking a player whether he had done enough practice. 'How could I?' came the reply. 'I had four shoots last week.' As proven by Brett Lee's guitar, the ability of cricketers in India to make their money from commodities other than runs, wickets and catches is unparalleled in the sport. In cynical old England, by contrast, we still snigger at the sight of cricketers behaving like celebrities and leaping onto advertising's gravy train. As *Private Eye* has pointed out, it just doesn't seem right seeing Matthew Hoggard, with his 'steadfast, indefatigable, son-of-the-soil persona', dressed up to the nines to alert the nation to the joys of Hugo Boss aftershave when he has already featured in a commercial for Marston's beer. 'So which is it to be, Hoggy,' wondered the *Eye*, 'yeoman or showman?' Or possibly just a sportsman with a limited shelf life keen to cash in before his body forces him to retire.

The new brand of Indians have no time for such coyness. They are not merely batsmen or bowlers. They are 'brand ambassadors'. When Sachin Tendulkar's five-year contract with WorldTel Sports came to an end in 2006, the race was on to manage his brand, a word used in Indian cricket circles without the slightest hint of embarrassment. In England, washing machines are brands. So are cars. Or possibly TV chefs. In India, it is all about cricketers, and usually about a 'marketable property' such as Sachin. 'You think you are mapping him, but he is mapping you,' a senior Indian executive told the journalist Deepak Mohanty. 'After you approach him, he begins to find out your financial strength. He asks you how you are going to position him and whether you can give him products that are appropriate to his standing. He is very smart. And, boy, is he connected.' The executive sounds like a frightened bowler, but then cricket and finance in India are so intertwined there were once rumours that some of their batsmen were on a pay-per-stay arrangement with their sponsors. The longer they hung around at the crease, accidentally thrusting the bat maker's name in front of the camera and drawing attention to the logos of the kit manufacturers with a few ostentatious rubs, the bigger the cheque. I could make a catty comment at this stage about the number of curious run-outs involving one or two Indians in recent times. But I won't.

The perception that, in India, money grows from stumps rather than on trees increased when it was announced that cricket's answer to football's Champions League, a Twenty20 competition involving eight of the best domestic sides in the world, would take place in late 2008. The total prize money would be a mind-boggling £2.5m. Now, India had their own domestic reasons for deciding to go ahead with this competition, not least to further undermine Kapil Dev's ICL. But the fact that India was now pumping resources into a form of the game they had previously objected to on the grounds that 50-over cricket presented far more opportunities for money-spinning commercial breaks, demonstrated their desire to remain at the cutting edge. (And now I'm starting to sound like a marketing man too . . .) Commentators agreed that cricket might never be the same again and they were aghast when the Texan billionaire Sir Allen Stanford dropped in to Lord's in a helicopter to announce his plans for a £10m game of Twenty20 between England and the West Indies in Antigua on 1 November 2008.

Take county cricket. Kent pocketed £42,000 for winning the 2007 Twenty20 Cup: they would stand to win almost twenty-four times as much if they managed to see off the competition in the Champions League. The county championship awarded £100,000 to its most recent winners – still a drop in the Indian Ocean. It does not need Nostradamus to work out in which direction counties who forever attract the tabloid tag 'cash-strapped' will head if a potential pot of gold awaits them every year. Yes, foreign cricketers have been heading to the county game for decades, lured not just by the prospect of honing their game in alien conditions but also by the strength of the pound. But this is on a different scale. When I visited the country for the opening fortnight of the IPL in April and May 2008, it was clear that foreign players now regarded India as the place to be.

In some ways, it's hard to credit. As John Wright pointed out: 'Although the BCCI generates a major proportion of cricket's total revenues, its office in Mumbai has concrete floors and a toilet that requires key access.' In other ways, it is perfectly believable. On the day India played Pakistan in the 2003 World Cup in Pakistan, Bill

Clinton was due in New York to speak via satellite to what Wright refers to as 'a high-powered conference in Delhi'. And how did they resolve this dilemma? 'They delayed his speech until the match finished.' Imagine a high-powered conference in London trying to pull the same stunt. It just wouldn't happen. Cricket has moved on from being the noble pastime so fondly envisaged by the English, with their wilfully backward-looking visions of old maids on bikes, village greens and foaming ale. In the last episode of the BBC TV comedy *Blackadder Goes Forth*, Captain Darling reflects on his impending doom after being summoned from his desk job to the trenches of the First World War. 'How are you feeling, Darling?' asks Blackadder as the soldiers prepare to go over the top. 'Ahm – not all that good, Blackadder,' he replies. 'Rather hoped I'd get through the whole show, go back to work at Pratt and Sons, keep wicket for the Croydon Gentlemen, marry Doris. Made a note in my diary on the way here. Simply says: "Bugger".' Even in a TV comedy set in 1917, cricket for the average Englishman is portrayed as a thing of nostalgia.

Perhaps one day, Indians will yearn for the peace and quiet of Twenty20, fondly recalling all the twists, turns and subtleties that are no longer part of the game in the middle of the 21st century. But for the moment, India cannot get enough of a sport which, spiritually and financially, is theirs for the taking.

ACKNOWLEDGEMENTS

Many people, most of them without knowing it, have contributed to this book but some deserve explicit thanks. My editor Tristan Jones helped cook up the idea and gently encouraged me to play my natural game. Jim Gill, my agent, was a reassuring source of sensible advice. Mike Peel lent me the priceless perspective of a fellow cricket nut; Tori Brown's eye was rarely less than aquiline. At various points, Andrew Miller, Altus Momberg, S. Rajesh, Siddhartha Vaidyananthan, Richard Boock and David Frith all helped out in one way or another, and I'm grateful to Jeremy Snape for waxing lyrical in his front room about the psychology of cricket (see Chapter 4). Thanks, too, to mum and dad for never once putting pressure on me to get a proper job: without their lack of discouragement, this book would never have appeared. And without a splendid effort by the whole team at Yellow Jersey Press it would not look as sharp as it does. Any prejudices that remain are entirely my own.